The Complete Dictionary of
INSURANCE TERMS

Explained Simply

By Melissa J. Samaroo

THE COMPLETE DICTIONARY OF INSURANCE TERMS EXPLAINED SIMPLY

Copyright © 2011 Atlantic Publishing Group, Inc.

1405 SW 6th Avenue • Ocala, Florida 34471 • Phone 352-622-1825 • Fax 352-622-1875

Web site: www.atlantic-pub.com • E-mail: sales@atlantic-pub.com

SAN Number: 268-1250

Library of Congress Cataloging-in-Publication Data

Samaroo, Melissa, 1982-
  The complete dictionary of insurance terms explained simply / by Melissa Samaroo.
    p. cm.
  Includes bibliographical references and index.
  ISBN-13: 978-1-60138-237-5 (alk. paper)
  ISBN-10: 1-60138-237-5 (alk. paper)
  1. Insurance--Dictionaries. I. Title.
  HG8025.S247 2010
  368.003--dc22

                        2010015886

PROJECT MANAGER: Kim Fulscher • PEER REVIEWER: Marilee Griffin
INTERIOR DESIGN: Samantha Martin
FRONT & BACK COVER DESIGN: Jackie Miller • millerjackiej@gmail.com

Printed in the United States

Over the years, we have adopted a number of dogs from rescues and shelters. First there was Bear and after he passed, Ginger and Scout. Now, we have Kira, another rescue. They have brought immense joy and love not just into our lives, but into the lives of all who met them.

We want you to know a portion of the profits of this book will be donated in Bear, Ginger and Scout's memory to local animal shelters, parks, conservation organizations, and other individuals and nonprofit organizations in need of assistance.

– Douglas & Sherri Brown,
President & Vice-President of Atlantic Publishing

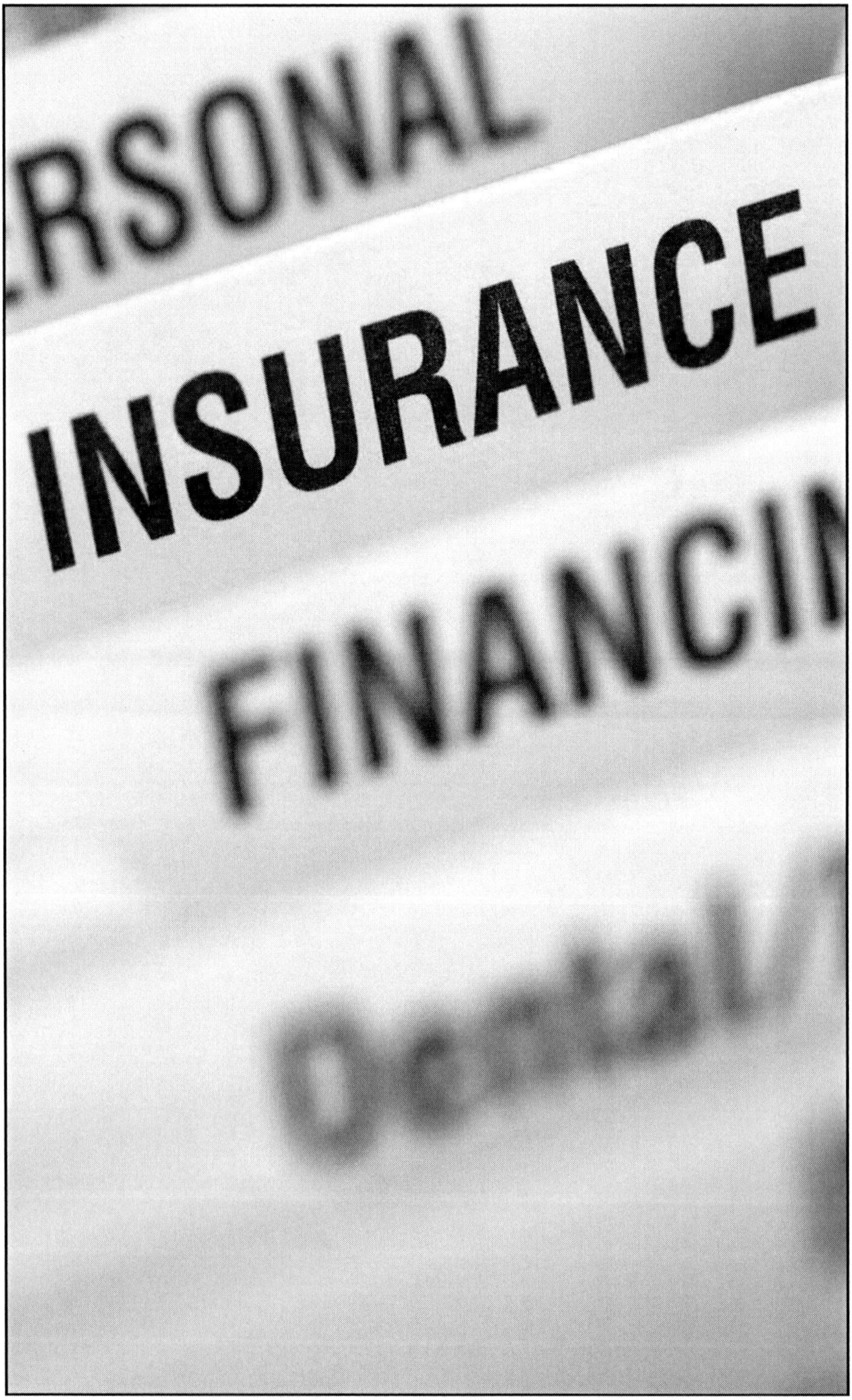
INSURANCE

DEDICATION

For Gabriel.

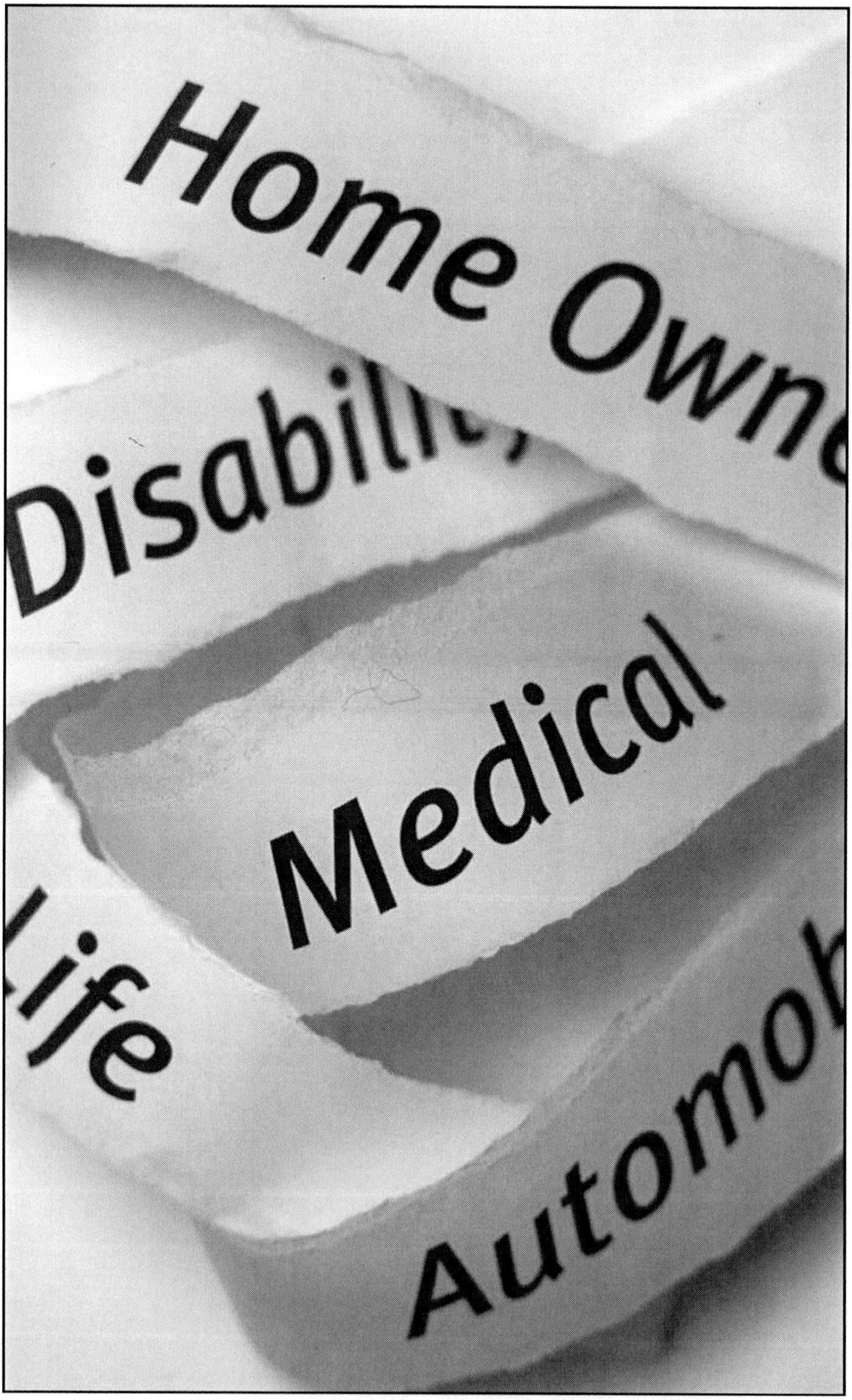
Home Owne
Disabilit
Medical
Life
Automob

CONTENTS

INTRODUCTION

Owning and operating a business is, in many ways, similar to being a first-time parent. Just like a new baby, the entity you have brought into the world needs your constant care and attention, all day. In both situations, many people find themselves ill-equipped and unprepared for the level of responsibility. Regardless of how you plan and prepare, many things can unexpectedly go wrong. When something catastrophic does happen, you must pick up the pieces in a timely manner and trudge forward. It is in those times that insurance can help the businessperson to salvage the situation.

As a business owner or working professional, the exposure to risk one faces can be enormous. There are an infinite number of situations in which an honest, hardworking person or partnership can face financial ruin due to a complete accident or simple oversight. Purchasing the right kind of insurance coverage in a sufficient amount can mean the difference between success and failure for a business owner. But this in itself is much more difficult than it seems. Insurance contracts are crammed with stipulations and fine print, and the terminology used in them is as foreign as another language. Using an insurance agent may be a wise course of action, but the added expense can mean the difference between a business turning a profit or recording a loss.

For those who find themselves in need of insurance coverage but mystified by the terminology, this book can be a cost-effective source of help. The terms commonly used by insurance companies, agents, and brokers are defined in simple language. The category or categories to which the term belongs are also listed directly before the definition, making it easy to interpret the different contexts in which the term may be used. Case studies from professionals in the insurance field also shed some light on the best way to approach determining your need for insurance, purchasing the coverage, and filing a claim.

Understanding insurance may seem tedious and difficult at first. But the joy of watching your business grown unhindered makes the effort worthwhile.

A

1035 exchange *(Life Insurance)* — As defined under section 1035a of the tax code, an exchange of life insurance for annuities.

24-hour care coverage *(Health Insurance/Workers Compensation)* — The blending of work-related and non-work-related benefits to offer 24-hour coverage for illnesses and injuries.

401h trust *(Health Insurance)* — A limited-use account used to fund employee insurance costs after retirement. Employer contributions are tax deductible and limited to an amount equal to 25 percent of contributions to retirement benefits.

401k plan *(Pensions)* — A retirement savings plan made up of employee contributions, taken from the employee's salary before tax. Employers may match the employee's contribution.

Abandonment clause *(Property Insurance)* — A stipulation that prevents the claimant from abandoning salvageable property with the intent of claiming a total loss.

Absolute liability *(General Insurance Terms)* — Liability associated with very dangerous actions. The actions leading to the liability do not have to be proven negligent, just different than public policy.

Acceleration life insurance *(Life Insurance)* — A policy that allows the insured to receive 25 percent of the death benefit before death. This is done in the case of certain medical conditions. The benefit is used on medical costs that will extend the insured's life. Any benefit that remains is paid out in the traditional manner, to the beneficiary, upon death.

Accident *(General Insurance Terms)* — An unplanned occurrence outside the control of the insured that happens suddenly and due to pure chance.

Accidental death and dismemberment insurance *(Health Insurance)* — Policy that pays out upon the insured's death due to an accident or incapacitating bodily injury.

Accredited advisor in insurance *(General Insurance Terms)* — An agent or other individual who has completed the three exams administered by the Insurance Institute of America.

Act of God *(General Insurance Terms)* — A natural event outside of any human control, such as an earthquake.

Actual cash value *(General Insurance Terms)* — Similar to market value; this amount is the cost of replacing damaged or destroyed items with new property. Consideration is given to the condition and depreciation of the item.

Additional death benefit *(Life Insurance)* — An extra benefit payable upon the insured's death.

Additional insured *(General Insurance Terms)* — A second beneficiary added to the same policy; for example, the children of the insured.

Additional living expense *(Property Insurance)* — Typically found in a homeowners policy. This coverage provides reimbursement of expenses incurred while the insured is forced to live outside his or her home temporarily; for example, the cost of temporary lodging or eating in restaurants.

Adhesion insurance contract *(General Insurance Terms)* — A contract offered on a "take-it-or-leave-it" basis.

Adjustable life insurance *(Life Insurance)* — A type of coverage wherein changes to the amount of policy, premium, period, or length are permitted.

Adjusted premium *(General Insurance Terms)* — A premium comprised of a net-level premium and an amount defined as the first year's acquisition expenses divided by the current value of a life annuity due.

Adjustment income *(Life Insurance)* — A benefit that provides an income to a beneficiary once the primary wage earner has died. This income is intended to help cover expenses until the beneficiary is self sufficient.

Adjustment provision *(General Insurance Terms)* — A stipulation in a policy that permits changes to the policy, which are then executed by increasing or decreasing the premium or face amount. Also can be changed by extending or decreasing the duration of protection or premiums.

Admitted company *(General Insurance Terms)* — A company licensed to provide insurance in a particular state.

Advance funding *(Pensions)* — Generally, designating money to fund future benefits. Commonly used in pensions to fund eventual retirement.

Adverse financial selection *(General Insurance Terms)* — When a policyholder surrenders the policy for cash due to financial need, or because the money can be better invested elsewhere.

Adverse selection *(General Insurance Terms)* — When an individual who is a higher-than-average risk tries to buy insurance at the standard rate.

Age setback *(Life Insurance)* — A practice based on the assumption that women outlive men and will be paying premiums for a longer period, wherein a number of years are subtracted from standard life insurance rates. This is considered a women's rights matter and has been brought to legislation in some states.

Age-weighted profit-sharing plan *(Life Insurance)* — A plan wherein larger contributions are made for older participants. After compound interest has been added, the smaller contribution made for the younger employee will equal the same retirement benefit as the larger one.

Agency by ratification *(General Insurance Terms)* — When the insurance company accepts the actions of an agent, this ratifies the act, making the company liable for consequences that may occur. For example, the insurance company is liable when they accept a premium on a policy the agent should not have sold.

Aggregate annual deductible *(General Insurance Terms)* — A deductible that applies for the entire year.

Aggregate indemnity *(Health Insurance)* — The maximum amount that may be claimed during a certain period or under the policy.

Aggregate limit *(General Insurance Terms)* — The maximum amount of coverage available to the insured during a certain period, regardless of the number of accidents during that period.

Agreed amount clause *(Property Insurance)* — A clause that stipulates that the amount of insurance will automatically meet the coinsurance clause.

Alien insurer *(General Insurance Terms)* — An insurer formed under the laws of a different country than the one it operates in.

Alliance of American Insurers *(General Insurance Terms)* — A group of insurers that work together in areas of common interest. For example, government affairs, education of employees, and loss prevention.

Allocated benefits *(Health Insurance)* — Payments with specific purposes, for example: supplies, drugs, or X-rays.

Alternative dispute resolution *(Health Insurance)* — Alternatives to the fee for service model, for example PPOs or HMOs. *See entries PPO and HMO.*

American agency system *(General Insurance Terms)* — Also known as the independent agency system, a system in which insurance is sold through independent agents.

American college *(Life Insurance)* — A college that does research related to life insurance and publishes the findings, in addition to continuing education for agents.

American Council of Life Insurance *(Life Insurance)* — Association of several insurance groups that exchange information, communicate, and are interested in legislative matters.

American Insurance Association *(General Insurance Terms)* — A group of property and liability insurance companies that promotes the standing of its members.

Amortization *(Pensions)* — A systematic process of paying a debt, with interest, over a given number of years.

Amortization schedule *(Pensions)* — A table detailing the schedule for paying off a debt over a given number of years.

Amount at risk *(Life Insurance)* — The difference between the given value of a life insurance policy and the cash value it has accrued. This is the amount the insurer would have to pay of his or her own money should the insured die and a death benefit need to be paid out.

Ancillary benefits *(Health Insurance)* — Coverage for charges associated with a hospital stay; for example, supplies, X-rays, and other diagnostic tests.

Annual aggregate limit *(General Insurance Terms)* — The yearly maximum that a policy will cover, regardless of how many claims are made.

Annual statement *(General Insurance Terms)* — A report of the insurer's finances submitted to the state insurance department.

Annuity *(Annuities)* — An amount payable annually, or an agreement for an insurer to make regular payments for a specific period.

Annuity analysis *(Annuities)* — An analysis that includes the annuity's interest rate and how long that rate is promised, the offering company's financial ranking, the expected monthly income, and other pertinent information.

Appearance allowance *(Vehicle Insurance)* — Money given to the insured to keep a part of the vehicle that is barely damaged.

Appleton rule *(General Insurance Terms)* — A rule requiring every insurer in New York to comply with the New York Insurance Code. If the insurer does business in any other state, he or she must still comply with this code.

Appointed actuary *(General Insurance Terms)* — An actuary appointed by an insurance company charged with documenting the liability reserve of an insurer.

Apportionment *(General Insurance Terms)* — A method of dividing a claim among more than one insurance company.

Apportionment clause *(Property Insurance)* — A clause that requires claims on a property to be divided among all insurance policies covering that property.

Appraisal *(General Insurance Terms)* — An assessment to determine the value of an item or property to obtain adequate insurance coverage or determine replacement value.

Appraisal clause *(Property Insurance)* — Clause that gives either party (the insured or the insurer) the right to an appraisal to determine the value of a loss.

Appurtenant structure *(Property Insurance)* — A secondary structure on the insured premises.

Arbitration clause *(Property Insurance)* — A clause stating that in case of a disagreement regarding the amount of a claim, each party (the insured and the insurer) will appoint an appraiser, who will then select an mediator. An amount will then be determined by at least two of these three, and this settlement will be binding.

Arson *(Legal Terminology)* — Intentional burning of property.

Assessable insurance *(General Insurance Terms)* — A policy under which a first premium is assessed and a second premium may be assessed later if the insurance company's losses exceed their premium income.

Assessed value *(General Insurance Terms)* — The value assigned to property by a government entity. This is done to establish the amount of taxes due on this property.

Assessment company *(General Insurance Terms)* — An insurer who may charge insured parties extra if the premiums already paid are not enough to cover their operating costs.

Assessment insurance *(General Insurance Terms)* — A policy wherein extra costs can be assessed to the policyholder should the insurer's loss experience be worse than expected.

Asset *(General Insurance Terms)* — An item of value listed on the balance sheet of an insurance company, for example, "property" or "office furniture."

Asset depreciation risk *(General Insurance Terms)* — The risk that the assets of a company may lose market value over time.

Asset valuation *(General Insurance Terms)* — The net profit or loss of a premium after deducting the insurance and expenses.

Asset valuation reserve *(General Insurance Terms)* — A reserve comprised of all invested assets of all classes. This reserve is made mandatory by the NAIC.

Assignment clause *(General Insurance Terms)* — A clause that allows the holder of a policy to sell or give the policy to another person or company.

Association or syndicate pool *(General Insurance Terms)* — A group of insurers who writes a large risk together and have an agreement to split the premiums and expenses. *See Risk.*

Assumed interest rate *(Annuities)* — A return on an immediate variable annuity that is calculated when the insurer determines the initial income payment.

Assumption of risk *(Legal Terminology)* — A concept in common law often used as a defense. Assumption of risk states that by certain actions, a person assumes certain risks. For example, by riding on the back of someone else's motorcycle, an individual has assumed the risk of a crash and should not be able to sue the driver should a crash occur.

Assumption reinsurance *(Reinsurance)* — A type of reinsurance. The company reinsuring the insured party assumes total responsibility for the policy from the original insurance company. This is done by transferring the policy from the insurer to the re-insurer.

Attained age *(Life Insurance)* — The age of the insured as of a certain date.

Attending physician statement *(Health Insurance/Life Insurance)* — A statement obtained from the individual's physician detailing the person's medical information. Typically used to write an insurance policy for the individual.

Attestation clause *(General Insurance Terms)* — A section that requires the officers of an insurance company to sign a contract for it to be completed.

Attractive nuisance *(Legal Terminology)* — Property that is deemed hazardous and appealing to children; for example, a swimming pool. Special precautions must be taken by the property owner to avoid liability.

Auto coverage *(Vehicle Insurance)* — An insurance policy providing coverage for a vehicle or trailer that operates on public roadways.

Automatic coverage *(General Insurance Terms)* — Coverage that is automatically provided under an existing policy to cover newly purchased property or property that appreciates in value.

Automatic increase in benefit provision *(Life Insurance)* — A clause found in disability coverage that increases the amount of payments by a previously stated percentage for a certain amount of years.

Automatic non-proportional reinsurance *(Reinsurance)* — Automatic protection of the insurer against losses that exceed a previously stated limit.

Automatic premium loan provision *(Life Insurance)* — A clause found in life insurance policies that states that any premium not paid at the end of the stated grace period will automatically be paid by a policy loan taken from the policy's cash value.

A

Automatic proportional reinsurance *(Reinsurance)* — A type of reinsurance wherein the insurer automatically reinsures certain risks with his or her reinsurer by transfer. Under this type of reinsurance, premiums and losses are divided between the insurer and reinsurer. The reinsurer pays the insurer a transfer commission.

Automatic reinstatement clause *(Property Insurance)* — A clause stating that the original policy limit will be reinstated after partial losses covered by the policy have been paid.

Automatic reinsurance *(Reinsurance)* — A type of reinsurance wherein the insurer automatically reinsures certain risks with a reinsurer. Both parties must accept this transfer.

Automobile assigned risk insurance plan *(Vehicle Insurance)* — A plan that provides automobile insurance to individuals otherwise unable to obtain coverage due to their driving records. The price of this type of insurance is higher than standard automobile coverage.

Automobile liability insurance *(Vehicle Insurance)* — Insurance that covers the insured in case of legal responsibility for damage caused by an automobile. Required by state law.

Automobile physical damage insurance *(Vehicle Insurance)* — Insurance that covers the insured's vehicle against damage caused by various sources; for example, vandalism or a fire.

Average earnings clause *(Life Insurance)* — Clause that states the beneficiary's disability payments can be reduced if his or her monthly income exceeds the total monthly earnings or the average monthly earnings. This is only valid within the first two years of the disability payments beginning.

Average semi-private rate *(Health Insurance)* — The average amount charged for a semi-private room in a hospital located in the area where the charge is made.

Average weekly wage *(Workers Compensation)* — The rate used to determine the amount of the insured's weekly benefits.

Aviation accident insurance *(Life Insurance)* — Insurance that covers passengers or pilots on a regularly scheduled airline.

Aviation exclusion *(Life Insurance)* — An exclusion that states the insured is not covered unless he or she is in a regularly scheduled airline. For example, the insured is not covered in the event of a small-plane crash.

Aviation hazard *(Aviation Insurance)* — The extra hazard that comes from the insured's participation in aviation or aeronautics.

Aviation insurance *(Aviation Insurance)* — Insurance that covers the insured in case of a loss stemming from the use of an airplane.

Aviation trip life insurance *(Life Insurance)* — A policy that covers the insured's life for the length of a specific flight.

B

Back load *(General Insurance Terms)* — Expenses deducted at the time benefits are paid out.

Backdating *(Health Insurance/Life Insurance)* — When the effective date of a policy is earlier than the application date. This is done so premiums can be calculated for a younger age than the insured's actual age.

Bailee *(Legal Terminology)* — A person entrusted with the belongings of another person.

Bailee's customers insurance *(Property Insurance)* — Insurance that covers the bailee, the person temporarily in possession of another's property, in case of damage to the property while under his care. The bailee is covered against many potential hazards, including fire damage, theft, robbery, and sprinkler leaks.

Bailment *(Legal Terminology)* — A person's property that has been temporarily entrusted to another person.

Bailor *(Legal Terminology)* — A person who has temporarily given his or her property over to another person.

Bank burglary and robbery insurance *(Liability Insurance)* — Insurance that covers the bank against theft or unauthorized taking of money or securities, as well as vandalism and damages arising from burglary or robbery.

Bankers blanket bond *(Criminal)* — Insurance that protects a bank against fraudulent acts perpetrated by employees, as well as theft or burglary perpetrated by non-employees.

Base premium *(General Insurance Terms)* — An insurance company's premium upon which the reinsurance premium is based.

Basic benefits *(Health Insurance)* — The minimum benefits provided by an insurance policy. Also called a basic hospital plan.

Basic form rates *(Property Insurance)* — As put forth under the commercial lines program, Group I and Group II rates combine to form the basic form rates.

Basic hospital plan *(Health Insurance)* — The minimum benefits provided by an insurance policy. Also called basic benefits.

Basic limit *(General Insurance Terms)* — The minimum amount for which a liability policy can be written.

Basic limits of liability *(General Insurance Terms)* — The minimum amount for which a liability policy can be written, as dictated by the published rates or the law.

Basic mortality table *(General Insurance Terms)* — A table listing the actual ages of death of a population, with no adjustments made for probability.

Basic premium *(General Insurance Terms)* — A fraction of the standard premium. This portion is used for administrative costs and agents' commissions.

Basic time frame *(Life Insurance)* — During the term of a life insurance policy, the time frame in which losses occur.

Beneficiary *(General Insurance Terms)* — The person designated to receive the benefits of a policy.

Beneficiary clause *(General Insurance Terms)* — Clause that allows the insured to designate anyone as a beneficiary, and to change this designation at any time.

Beneficiary of trust *(General Insurance Terms)* — A person for whom a trust has been created and who will eventually receive the benefits of said trust.

Benefit *(General Insurance Terms)* — An amount paid to a beneficiary of an insurance policy, or the participant of a retirement plan.

Benefit allocation method *(Pensions)* — A method of funding a pension. Only one premium payment is made per year and used to purchase a single benefit. This is done for each year of service to the employer. Usually, an annuity is purchased.

Benefit formula *(Health Insurance)* — A way of calculating the amount of benefits the insured is entitled to, under an employee benefit plan.

Benefit period *(Health Insurance)* — The time frame in which money or other policy benefits are paid out to either the insured or the insured's dependents.

B

Benefit triggers *(Health Insurance)* — Conditions to be met before benefits are paid out.

Binder *(General Insurance Terms)* — A temporary measure that provides coverage before a contract is finalized or before premiums are paid.

Binding receipt *(Property Insurance)* — Proof of a temporary contract, which forces a property insurance company to provide coverage, provided that a premium is paid with the application. *For the definition as it applies to health or life insurance, see Conditional receipt.*

Binomial distribution *(General Insurance Terms)* — A function used to predict the probability of future events.

Blackout period *(Life Insurance)* — The time frame between when a deceased person's spouse stops receiving survivor benefits and when he or she begins receiving retirement benefits.

Blanket bond *(Criminal)* — A fidelity bond covering losses caused by the dishonest acts of any employee.

Blanket contract *(Health Insurance)* — *See blanket insurance.*

Blanket coverage *(Health Insurance)* — *See blanket insurance.*

Blanket crime policy *(Criminal)* — A policy providing coverage for dishonest employees, loss of money orders, depositor's forgery, or counterfeit currency. This type of policy has been replaced by commercial crime coverage or the commercial package policy.

Blanket insurance *(Health Insurance/Property Insurance)* — A health insurance contract that covers an entire group of people without identifying each individually. In property insurance, a contract that covers either multiple types of property at one location or several types of property at multiple locations.

Blanket limit *(General Insurance Terms)* — Maximum amount of coverage that a company will write in a particular area.

Blanket medical expense insurance *(Health Insurance)* — Policy that covers medical costs, except for certain specific exclusions.

Blanket rate *(Property Insurance)* — The amount of premiums charged for blanket insurance covering properties at more than one location.

Blended insurance program *(General Insurance Terms)* — A long-term program that combines many types of insurance including finite risk, reinsurance, and traditional insurance.

Blending *(Life Insurance)* — The act of merging a term life insurance policy with an ordinary life insurance policy.

Block limits *(Property Insurance)* — Maximum amount of insurance that an insurance company will write on a specific city block.

Block of policies *(General Insurance Terms)* — The total number of policies written by one insurance company using the same policy forms and rates.

Blue Cross *(Health Insurance)* — A hospital expense plan that provides coverage for hospital treatment with some specific restrictions, for example, the type of room occupied. Blue Cross and Blue Shield are both under the same national federation of independently owned companies. Blue Cross covers hospital

B

expenses, and Blue Shield covers medical and surgical costs. *See Blue Shield.*

Blue Shield *(Health Insurance)* — A medical or surgical expense plan. Blue Cross and Blue Shield are both under the same national federation of independently owned companies. Blue Cross covers hospital expenses, and Blue Shield covers medical and surgical costs.

Bobtail liability insurance *(Liability)* — Insurance that covers commercially used tractor trailor trucks returning to a terminal after depositing cargo elsewhere.

Bodily injury *(Health Insurance)* — Physical damage to a person's body.

Bond *(General Insurance Terms)* — A contract between three parties: a principal, a surety, and an obligee. The bond is issued by the surety and promises the obligee financial protection in case the principal fails to perform a duty or is found to be dishonest.

Book of business *(General Insurance Terms)* — A book totaling all insurance written by a company or agent.

Book value *(General Insurance Terms)* — The cash value of the company's assets as listed on the company's accounting records.

Boot *(General Insurance Terms)* — Consideration for a tax-free transfer of property; usually money or other property.

Bordereau *(Reinsurance)* — Reinsurance where the ceding company provides certain information to the reinsurer. The ceding company gets the loss history and history of premiums as they pertain to certain risks.

Borderline risk *(General Insurance Terms)* — An applicant of doubtful quality, according to underwriting standards.

Borrowing Authority of Pension Benefit Guaranty Corporation *(PBGC) (Pensions)* — A pension benefit guaranty corporation that has been granted authorization to borrow from the United States Treasury. This is done through issuance of Treasury notes.

Boston plan *(Property Insurance)* — An ongoing plan under which insurers have agreed not to reject providing coverage to residences in slum areas. Coverage is extended until there has been an inspection and the owner has had a chance to correct imperfections. Called the "Boston plan" because Boston was the first to offer such a plan.

Bottomry *(Property Insurance)* — An insurance contract that accepts a ship or its cargo as collateral for a loan funding a maritime voyage. In the event the ship is lost at sea, the loan is cancelled and the borrower is not obligated to repay the lender.

Breach of contract *(Legal Terminology)* — Failure of one of the parties of a contract to meet contractual obligations.

Bridge insurance *(Property Insurance)* — Insurance that covers a structural bridge in the event of damage or destruction.

Bridge insurance for bridges under construction *(Property Insurance)* — Insurance that covers a bridge against fire damage, lightning strike, earthquake, collision, flood, and other acts of God while the bridge is in the process of construction.

B

Broad evidence rule *(Property Insurance)* — Rule applied to calculating the actual cash value of lost property. Under this rule, any evidence about the value of the item is considered admissible. The item's value can also be determined by any means that accurately depicts its true value.

Broad form cause of loss *(Property Insurance)* — A type of homeowners insurance wherein most reasons for a loss are covered.

Broad form *(Liability/Property Insurance)* — Insurance that covers many hazards to include theft, loss, property damage, and vandalism.

Broad form personal theft insurance *(Criminal)* — Usually part of a homeowner's insurance policy; this type of policy covers theft at a private residence. This type of coverage usually protects against all perils such as vandalism, theft, and damages occurring due to malicious mischief.

Broad form property damage endorsement *(Liability)* — An addition to a general liability policy that negates the exclusion of property in the care or custody of the insured.

Broad form storekeepers insurance *(Criminal)* — Insurance that covers owners of small stores against burglary, robbery, depositor forgery, or employee dishonesty.

Broker *(General Insurance Terms)* — A person who acts on behalf of another to obtain insurance. They may also represent the insurer in a limited capacity, for example, to collect premiums.

Broker agent *(General Insurance Terms)* — A person who acts as a broker for some insurers and an agent for others.

Brokerage *(General Insurance Terms)* — The sum paid to a broker as a commission. This term can also refer to insurance placed with brokers.

Brokerage business *(General Insurance Terms)* — Business brought in by a broker to an insurance company.

Brokerage department *(General Insurance Terms)* — The department within an insurer places insurance with brokers.

Brokerage fee *(General Insurance Terms)* — The fee earned by a broker for selling a company's insurance.

Brokerage general agent *(General Insurance Terms)* — An independent agent who sells the insurance company's products to brokers, so the brokers can then sell them to the public. This person is charged with appointing brokers on behalf of the company.

Brokerage supervisor *(General Insurance Terms)* — An insurance company employee authorized to designate insurance company brokers.

Builder's risk coverage forms *(Property Insurance)* — Insurance coverage for buildings currently under construction.

Bureau insurer *(General Insurance Terms)* — An insurance company that has joined a rating bureau, usually due to a lack of insurance company experience in a certain type of risk.

Burglary *(Criminal)* — A felony crime defined as the forcible breaking and entering into someone else's property.

B

Burglary insurance *(Criminal)* — Insurance against losses caused by a burglary.

Burning cost ratio *(Reinsurance)* — The ratio of losses that an insurer has to cover by contract to premium income. In an excess of loss or catastrophe loss reinsurance policy, premium income is defined as gross premium minus reinsurance expenses. For stop loss reinsurance policies, premium income is defined as earned premium income.

Burning ratio *(General Insurance Terms)* — The amount of losses suffered as compared to the amount of insurance in effect.

Business and personal property coverage form *(Property Insurance)* — Coverage for buildings and property contained within them.

Business auto coverage form *(Vehicle Insurance)* — A policy covering commercial automobiles against damage and liability, which has largely replaced the business automobile policy.

Business automobile policy *(Vehicle Insurance)* — A policy covering commercial automobiles against damage and liability. Replaced by the business auto coverage form in most areas.

Business crime insurance *(Criminal)* — Insurance that covers the business' assets against forgery, robbery, and embezzlement.

Business income coverage form *(Property Insurance)* — A form that provides coverage against losses that occur due to property damage, for example, loss of business.

Business insurance *(General Insurance Terms)* — Insurance written for businesses. Can refer to health insurance or life insurance written for the principals of a company.

Business interruption *(Liability Insurance)* — Interruption of day-to-day dealings by a business due to a loss.

Business interruption insurance *(Liability Insurance)* — Insurance that covers lost income due to an interruption in business caused by a covered loss.

Business liability insurance *(Liability Insurance)* — Coverage provided to a business owner against property damage, personal injury, fire damage, and bodily injury.

Business life and health insurance *(Liability Insurance)* — Insurance that assists in funding the day-to-day operation of a business in the event a key person is lost.

Business property and liability insurance package *(Property Insurance)* — Insurance for business-owned property against damage or loss by fire or vandalism. Also covers bodily injury or damage to the property of others caused by representatives of the business.

Business risk *(General Insurance Terms)* — A risk to the company's earning capability.

Business risk exclusion *(General Insurance Terms)* — An exclusion that omits coverage for sub-par products that do not work as well as the insured had promised.

B

Business owner's policy *(Liability/Property Insurance)* — A policy that provides liability and property coverage for small businesses.

Buy-sell agreement *(Liability)* — An agreement that states if a part-owner of a business wishes to sell, he or she must sell to the other part-owners or another person named in the agreement. The price of the part of the business is also named in the agreement.

Buy-back deductible *(General Insurance Terms)* — A deductible that can be eliminated by the payment of an extra premium.

C

Cafeteria benefit plan *(Health Insurance)* — A plan that allows employees to choose the allocation of their premiums and the composition of their benefits.

Calendar year deductible *(Health Insurance)* — A deductible that must be met in a calendar year, no matter how many claims are made.

Cancel *(General Insurance Terms)* — The ending of a policy, as dictated by the terms of the contract.

Cancellation provision clause *(Property/Health Insurance)* — A clause that grants either party the right to terminate the policy at any time before the expiration date.

Capacity *(General Insurance Terms)* — The largest quantity of insurance or reinsurance available for purchase, either from one company or from the entire market.

Capacity of parties *(General Insurance Terms)* — Legal competency of each party to enter in a contract.

C

Captive agent *(General Insurance Terms)* — An agent who represents one insurance company exclusively.

Captive insurance company *(General Insurance Terms)* — A company formed exclusively to insure a parent company.

Care, custody, and control *(Liability)* — A category of property typically excluded in liability policies. Items considered to be in the care, custody, and control of the insured are typically not covered by liability policies because they either belong to the insured and are therefore better covered under property insurance, or the item is with the insured because he or she is the bailor of this property. In that case, the property is better covered under a bailor or baillee's insurance form.

Cargo insurance *(Property Insurance)* — Insurance that covers cargo as it is transported to another location.

Carpenter plan *(Reinsurance)* — A reinsurance plan wherein the premium is determined by the amount of the insurance company's losses during a period of time.

Carrier *(General Insurance Terms)* — Another term for insurer. Insurer is used more often because carrier can also mean a transportation carrier.

Cash accumulation method *(Life Insurance)* — Method of comparing the cost of life insurance policies with the same death benefit. The differences between the premiums paid to each policy are kept and accumulate interest at a given rate. At the end of a predetermined time frame, the largest amount accumulated from the difference of premiums paid is considered the most cost effective.

Cash flow plans *(General Insurance Terms)* — A method of paying premiums under which the insured keeps a portion of the premium and pays the premium out over a given time frame.

Cash flow underwriting *(General Insurance Terms)* — A method of maximizing interest earned on premiums through rating and premium collection.

Cash out of vested benefits *(General Insurance Terms)* — Money taken out of benefits by an employee.

Cash surrender value *(Liability Insurance)* — The amount of money due upon surrender of cash value life insurance.

Cash value life insurance *(Life Insurance)* — A life insurance policy that accumulates a savings.

Cash withdrawals *(Life Insurance)* — Removing cash from a policy or an employee benefit plan. This reduces the total death benefit by the amount of the cash withdrawal plus interest. In the case of an employee benefit plan, a withdrawal may mean forfeiture of employer-purchased benefits.

Casualty *(General Insurance Terms)* — A loss incurred due to an accident.

Casualty catastrophe *(General Insurance Terms)* — A large loss due to an accident.

Casualty insurance *(Liability)* — Insurance that covers the legal responsibility for losses stemming from damage to another's property or an injury to someone's person.

C

Catastrophe futures *(General Insurance Terms)* — A financial instrument purchased by insurance companies as a form of protection against large-scale future losses

Catastrophe hazard *(General Insurance Terms)* — The danger of a large-scale loss due to a hazard that could affect a very large number of insured people; for example, an earthquake.

Catastrophe loss *(General Insurance Terms)* — A difficult-to-predict, severe loss that is best covered by an insurance company; for example, an earthquake or hurricane.

Cease and desist order *(Legal Terminology)* — A court order that requires a company or individual to stop a certain act or practice. This order can also come from the state's insurance commissioner.

Cause of loss form *(General Insurance Terms)* — A form attached to a commercial policy that lists specific causes of loss to be covered by that policy.

Cede *(Reinsurance)* — The act of transferring insurance or reinsurance from an insurer to a reinsurer. Can also refer to buying reinsurance.

Ceding company *(Reinsurance)* — The insurance company that transfers the insurance it has written to another insurance company.

Certificate of authority *(Health Insurance)* — A state-issued certificate licensing the operation of a health maintenance organization.

Certified financial planner *(General Insurance Terms)* — A person who has passed several national exams and been designated by the International Board of Standards and Practices for Certified Financial Planners.

Cestui que vie *(General Insurance Terms)* — From the French, literally "he or she who lives." Also called the insured or the policyholder. The person whose life measures the duration of a trust, gift, estate, or insurance contract.

Change in occupancy or use clause *(Property Insurance)* — A change in the use of the premises that increases the possible risk. Once an insurance company receives notice of such a change, it may then increase the premiums or cancel the insurance policy.

Change of beneficiary provision *(General Insurance Terms)* — A provision that permits the insured to change the beneficiary as often as he or she wishes, except in policies where the beneficiary is irrevocable. In the case of an irrevocable beneficiary, the beneficiary must provide written consent for a change to be made.

Channeling *(Health Insurance)* — A hospital insurance policy that covers unemployed hospital physicians in the case of medical professional liability. This is done to tie physicians to a particular hospital and increase patient admissions to the hospital.

Chargeable *(Vehicle Insurance)* — Term for vehicle accidents that are found to be the fault of the insured and are attributed to the insured's driving record.

Charitable gift life insurance *(Life Insurance)* — Policy donated to a charity. The charity can borrow against the policy's cash value, surrender the policy for the cash value, or convert it from a group to an individual policy. The donor recieves a tax deduction.

Churning *(Life Insurance)* — The unnecessary replacement of life insurance policies that already exist to earn extra commissions. This practice is illegal.

Choice no-fault plan *(Vehicle Insurance)* — The choice of a vehicle owner to be covered under a no-fault plan provided by the state.

Chronically ill individual *(Health Insurance)* — An individual certified as lacking a physical or mental ability required to live independently. This certification must be made by a medical professional or social worker.

Civil wrong *(General Insurance Terms)* — An act comprised of two parts. The first, called a tort, is an act against another person or their property. The second is the breach of the terms of a contract.

Civilian Health and Medical Program of the Uniformed Services *(Health Insurance)* — Former name for the health insurance provided to family members of military members. This insurance only covers mandatory care and services.

Claim *(General Insurance Terms)* — A request for disbursement of the benefits promised in the contract.

Claim agent *(General Insurance Terms)* — An agent of the insurance company who has the power to pay the insured for a loss.

Claim department *(General Insurance Terms)* — The insurance company's department that assesses whether claims will be paid.

Claim expense *(General Insurance Terms)* — The costs, other than the actual claim cost, that are associated with paying a claim.

Claim provision *(General Insurance Terms)* — A clause outlining the process of submitting and administrating claims.

Claim report *(General Insurance Terms)* — A report compiled by an agent detailing the specifics of a claim.

Claimant *(General Insurance Terms)* — The individual requesting payment of a claim.

Claims made basis liability coverage *(Liability Insurance)* — Under this type of coverage, claims submitted during the term of a liability policy must be paid, even if the event causing the claim did not occur during the term.

Claims occurrence basis liability coverage *(Liability Insurance)* — Under this type of coverage, claims caused by an event that occurred during the term of a liability policy must be paid, even if the claim is not submitted during the term of the policy.

Claims reserve *(General Insurance Terms)* — Money designated to cover the claims that have occurred but have not yet been settled.

Class *(General Insurance Terms)* — A group of policyholders who have the same characteristics and are grouped together to be rated.

Class rate *(Property Insurance)* — A rate for risks grouped into the same class, that is, risks of the same danger.

Clause *(General Insurance Terms)* — A portion of a contract that speaks to a specific issue.

Cleanup fund *(Life Insurance)* — A fund or policy used to pay the remaining costs stemming from the policyholder's death.

Clear space clause *(Property Insurance)* — A clause stating that the insured's belongings must be stored at a specified distance from each other or other belongings. The property in question typically increases the chance of a loss, for example, dynamite or stacks of firewood near a firepit.

Coinsurance *(Property Insurance/Health Insurance)* — In property insurance, a formula that outlines the portion of each claim that the insurance company will pay. In health insurance, the term refers to the policyholder's portion of covered medical costs.

Coinsurance cap *(Health Insurance)* — Under coinsurance, a cap placed on the amount the policyholder must pay.

Coinsurance limit *(General Insurance Terms)* — The amount of coverage mandated by the coinsurance clause in an open stock burglary policy.

Coinsurance penalty *(General Insurance Terms)* — A penalty taken out of the figure the policyholder is given by the insurance company for a property loss. This penalty is assessed due to the insurance company failing to carry enough coverage, as detailed in the coinsurance clause.

Coinsurance percentage *(Property Insurance)* — A condition in a property insurance policy that makes the policyholder to have insurance as a percentage of the property's value. If this insurance does not exist, the policyholder is charged the coinsurance penalty.

Coinsurance plan of reinsurance *(Reinsurance)* — A kind of reinsurance, where the insurance company gives a segment of the life insurance policy it has written to the reinsurer. The reinsurer must pay some fraction of the death benefit to the insurance company upon the policy holder's death. The insurance company must then pay the beneficiary.

Coinsurance requirement *(General Insurance Terms)* — The total amount of insurance the policyholder must possess so he or she can be covered for the total amount of a loss and not be charged the coinsurance penalty.

Coinsurer *(General Insurance Terms)* — Under an insurance policy, someone who shares in the loss.

Collateral assignment *(Life Insurance)* — Use of a life insurance policy to secure a loan. Should the policyholder default on the loan, the creditor could recoup the interest on the loan from the policy.

Collateral creditor *(General Insurance Terms)* — A person who has been appointed the rights to a benefit.

Collection commission *(Life Insurance)* — A portion of the premiums gathered on debt insurance, paid to the agent who collected them.

Collection fee *(Life Insurance)* — A fee paid to an insurance agent for collecting policy premiums.

Collision *(Vehicle Insurance)* — Impact between a vehicle with another object, causing damage to the insured vehicle.

C

Collision damage waiver *(Vehicle Insurance)* — Special policy for individuals who have rented a vehicle. Under this policy, the rental company waives the right to collect damages from the individual for any loss, even if the individual is at fault. There is a sizable fee associated with this coverage.

Collision insurance *(Vehicle Insurance)* — Insurance that covers the insured in case of damage to his or her vehicle as the result of a collision.

Combination agency *(Life Insurance)* — An agency that sells both life insurance and industrial life insurance.

Combination agent *(Life Insurance)* — An agent who sells industrial life insurance and regular life insurance.

Combination plan *(Life Insurance)* — Combining life insurance with a side fund or auxiliary fund to increase the amount of money available to a pension or annuity in the future.

Combination policy *(Vehicle Insurance)* — A type of policy that is no longer popular; made up of multiple contracts written by multiple insurers.

Combined ratio *(General Insurance Terms)* — An expense ratio combined with a loss ratio. In underwriting, a loss occurs if the combined ratio is under 100 percent and a profit occurs if the combined ratio is over 100 percent.

Combined single limit *(General Insurance Terms)* — Total liability due to bodily injury and property damage combined, as one single sum of coverage.

Commencement of coverage *(General Insurance Terms)* —
Date that insurance coverage begins.

Commercial blanket bond *(General Insurance Terms)* — Blanket coverage of employees supplied by the employer. Under this type of coverage, the maximum loss limit is applied to any loss regardless of how many people were involved in the loss.

Commercial credit insurance *(General Insurance Terms)* —
Coverage that insures a manufacturing or service organization firm in the case of its debtors defaulting on debts owed.

Commercial crime coverage form *(Property Insurance)* —
Insurance that covers a business against 18 different types of loss. These are separated into different forms, each briefly described as follows:

- *Form A* covers employee dishonesty concerning money or properties.
- *Form B* covers forgery or falsification of monetary instruments.
- *Form C* covers against theft.
- *Form D* protects against robbery or safe burglary.
- *Form E* is for burglary of a business location.
- *Form F* covers fraud by computer.
- *Form G* covers extortion.
- *Form H* is for theft of items other than money and securities at the business location.
- *Form I* covers the loss of items in a safe deposit box due to theft.

C

- *Form J* covers securities deposited with a guardian.

- *Form K* is for liability for a guest's property left in a safe deposit box.

- *Form L* covers other liability to the guest's property.

- *Form M* covers liability for a safe depository.

- *Form N* further covers safe depository loss.

- *Form O* covers dishonesty of public employees. This can include dishonesty and misrepresentation.

- *Form P* further covers dishonesty of public employees.

- *Form Q* covers robbery of money and security.

- *Form R* covers acts conducted by using false monetary instruments.

Commercial forgery policy *(General Insurance Terms)* — Insurance that covers a business that unwittingly takes a forged check as payment.

Commercial forms *(General Insurance Terms)* — A form that offers insurance against many business risks.

Commercial health insurance *(Health Insurance)* — Insurance that provides coverage of both medical costs and disability benefits. This type of insurance is identifiable due to the existence of renewal provisions and the provision of benefits.

Commercial insurance *(General Insurance Terms)* — Coverage sold by insurance companies with the intent of making a profit.

Commercial insurance company *(General Insurance Terms)* — A company owned by private citizens, selling insurance to make a profit.

Commercial lines *(General Insurance Terms)* — Insurance sold to businesses and other commercial entities.

Commercial lines manual *(General Insurance Terms)* — A manual compiled by the Insurance Services Office Inc. that includes data on commercial rates. This manual is used to help determine rates.

Commercial package policy *(General Insurance Terms)* — Insurance coverage for a commercial organization that covers at least two of the following: Commercial Property, Business Crime, Business Automobile, Boiler and Machinery, Commercial General Liability, Inland Marine, Farmowners, and Ranchowners.

Commercial property floater *(General Insurance Terms)* — A way to insure a business that does not operate from one fixed location; for example, a food vendor that changes location or sells at different events.

Commercial property policy *(General Insurance Terms)* — Insurance that covers risks associated with operating a business; for example fire, burglary, or theft.

Commission of authority *(General Insurance Terms)* — The power designated to an agent by an insurance company.

Commissioner of insurance *(General Insurance Terms)* — At the state level, the highest regulator of insurance, elected to protect the interests of the policy owner.

C

Commissioner's standard industrial mortality table *(Life Insurance)* — A table used to find the nonforfeiture value due to the policyholder of an industrial life insurance policy.

Commissioner's standard ordinary mortality table *(Life Insurance)* — A table used to find the nonforfeiture value due to the policyholder of a life insurance policy.

Commissioner's values *(General Insurance Terms)* — A list of the values of securities published by the national association of insurance commissioners annually. This list is used when documenting the values of the securities owned by the insurance company on its balance sheet.

Common disaster clause *(Life Insurance)* — A clause used to establish the procedure of paying out on the policy, should the insured and his or her beneficiary die at the same time.

Commutation *(Life Insurance)* — The trade of a series of payments for a lump sum settlement.

Commutation right *(Life Insurance)* — The beneficiary's right to exchange a series of payments for a lump sum.

Comparative negligence *(Legal Terminology)* — A concept within tort law that applies in some states. The concept states that the negligence of both people involved in an accident is proportional to their contribution to the accident.

Compensating balances plan *(General Insurance Terms)* — A plan wherein premiums are paid by a business to the insurance company. The insurance company then deposits the premium, minus some costs, into a bank account in the insured's name. The insured business can make withdrawals from these funds.

Compensatory damages *(Legal Terminology)* — Damages awarded to the insured for a loss or injury he or she has suffered. This may include damages given for mental or physical suffering, time lost, or expenses.

Competence *(Legal Terminology)* — The mental capacity to understand the consequences of entering a contract. This is required to enter a contract with an insurer.

Completed operations insurance *(Liability Insurance)* — Insurance that covers contractors for liability stemming from accidents that occur due to the contractor completing a job.

Comprehensive general liability insurance *(Liability Insurance)* — Insurance that covers several possible liabilities including: completed operations, owner's protective, products liability, and premises and operations.

Comprehensive glass insurance *(Property)* — Insurance that covers glass breaking for almost any reason, for example the shattering of a store's windows.

Comprehensive health insurance *(Health Insurance)* — Total coverage for health care-related charges. This coverage is after deductibles and co-insurance are applied to any hospital or physician's office visit costs.

Comprehensive insurance *(General Insurance Terms/Vehicle Insurance)* — A general term meaning an insurance policy that covers a large variety of circumstances. In vehicle insurance, a

C

policy that covers loss or damage due to causes other than collision; for example, theft, fire, or vandalism.

Composite rate *(Vehicle Insurance/Liability Insurance)* — A single rate for which the insured is covered against a variety of perils. This is done to make it easier to calculate the premiums.

Comprehensive Medicare supplement *(Health Insurance)* — A policy that covers the deductible and co-insurance amount due for treatment under Medicare.

Comprehensive personal liability insurance *(Liability Insurance)* — Insurance that covers individuals in their private lives, as opposed to their professional lives, against liability stemming from accidents.

Comprehensive policy *(Vehicle Insurance/Liability Insurance)* — A policy covering all risks with exclusions named in the contract.

Compulsory insurance *(General Insurance Terms)* — A general term for insurance made mandatory by law; for example, automobile insurance.

Concealment *(Legal Terminology)* — The act of concealing a material fact.

Concurrency *(General Insurance Terms)* — When two policies provide the same coverage for the same risk.

Concurrent causation *(General Insurance Terms)* — A loss brought about by at least two events. In recent years, concurrent causation has been controversial as one event may be covered but the other not covered.

Condition *(General Insurance Terms)* — An action that must be completed to have the insurance policy remain valid and for claims to be paid. For example, the policy's premiums must be paid up to date.

Condition subsequent *(General Insurance Terms)* — A stipulation in the policy that will cause the contract to be invalid, should a certain event take place.

Conditional *(General Insurance Terms)* — In the insurance contract, the terms that outline the conditions necessary to keep the policy valid.

Conditional receipt *(Life Insurance/Health Insurance)* — Proof of an interim contract, which forces a health or life insurance company to pay out benefits as long as an adequate application and a premium were received.

Conditions for qualification *(General Insurance Terms)* — The duties required of the insured before benefits are paid; for example, submitting an inventory of items lost.

Condominium insurance *(Property Insurance)* — Homeowners insurance covering the insured's property against many perils, including fire, robbery, vandalism, smoke, and explosion.

Confining condition *(Health Insurance)* — An illness or disability that forces the insured to remain confined at home or in a medical facility.

Consequential loss *(Property Insurance)* — An indirect loss caused by the insured not being able to use his or her property. This type of loss does not happen right away; for example, busi-

C

ness interruption. This term can also refer to a loss caused by a hazard the insured is not directly insured for. For example, the spoilage of food due to power outage.

Conservation *(General Insurance Terms)* — An attempt by the insurer to retain current policies by not allowing them to lapse. For example, calling the customer or sending a reminder that payment should be made before a certain date or coverage will lapse.

Conservator *(General Insurance Terms)* — A person selected by the court or other legal authority to direct and manage an insurance company found to be in danger of failure.

Consideration *(General Insurance Terms)* — A trade of something of value, which becomes the basis of a contract. In the case of insurance, the consideration is the premium paid by the insured and the future payout of claims by the insurance company.

Construction insurance *(Property Insurance)* — Insurance that covers damage to or destruction of a building while construction is in progress.

Contents *(Property Insurance)* — In personal property insurance, contents refers to property that belongs to the insured and is separate from the home; for example, electronics, clothing, and furnishings. The term does not apply to pets, crops, boats, or vehicles. In commercial property insurance, contents refers to the business's property that is separate from the business's building; for example, office furniture, computers, or machinery.

Contents rate *(General Insurance Terms)* — The rate of the premium charged for the contents of a building, but not the actual building structure.

Contingency *(General Insurance Terms)* — An occurrence that may or may not take place within a certain time frame.

Contingency reserve *(General Insurance Terms)* — A reserve set aside for unforeseen events or damages. Found in the insurance company's annual statement.

Contingent beneficiary *(Life Insurance)* — A secondary beneficiary, named to receive the benefits of the policy if the primary beneficiary is deceased at the time of payout.

Contingent commission *(Reinsurance)* — A commission based on the net profit taken from a reinsurance treaty, paid to the ceding company in addition to the usual commission.

Contingent fund *(General Insurance Terms)* — A fund set aside for possible losses incurred as a result of a rare event.

Contingent liability *(Liability)* — A liability for which a person, partnership, or company may be responsible, even though the liability was caused by non-employees.

Continuation *(Health Insurance)* — A way for former employees to continue the health insurance they were covered under. The former employee must meet certain conditions.

Continuing care retirement communities *(Health Insurance)* — Communities where residents have easy access to health care.

Continuing education requirement *(General Insurance Terms)* — A required minimum amount of insurance-related education that license holders must complete to renew their licenses. Enforced by the state.

C

Continuous premium whole life policy *(Life Insurance)* — A life insurance policy that spreads premium payments throughout the duration of the insured's life, up to age 100.

Contract *(General Insurance Terms)* — The agreement between the insured and the insurer, wherein it is agreed that consideration will be traded for benefits and services. This term can also mean the agreement between an insurer and the agency he or she works with.

Contract of adhesion *(General Insurance Terms)* — A contract that cannot be bargained over. Insurance contracts are considered contracts of adhesion because the insured cannot negotiate the terms.

Contract of insurance *(Legal Terminology)* — The contract wherein the insurer agrees to provide benefits or services to the insured.

Contract year *(Health Insurance)* — The time from the effective date to the expiration date is considered the contract year.

Contract carrier *(Property Insurance)* — A company that transports the merchandise of certain merchants only, as opposed to a carrier who will carry cargo for the general public.

Contractual liability insurance *(Liability)* — Insurance that covers the insured against liabilities they are responsible for as stated in a written contract.

Contributing location *(Property)* — One of the four categories of properties covered under business income insurance. A property used to supply equipment or assistance.

Contribution *(General Insurance Terms)* — A term that can have several meanings in the context of insurance. A contribution can be the portion of a loss paid by each insurer, when two or more cover the same loss. Or the term can mean the portion of a premium paid by the insured. The term can also mean the portion of the loss paid by the insurer under coinsurance.

Contribution formula *(Pensions)* — A formula that outlines the amount the employer will pay into a profit sharing plan. The formula can also be for a money purchase plan.

Contributory *(Health Insurance/Life Insurance)* — A classification used to denote any employee coverage plan in which the employee contributes at least a portion of the premium.

Contributory negligence *(Legal Terminology)* — A legal concept stating that the insured may have contributed to his or her own injury. This may be because he or she did not take proper precautions.

Control *(General Insurance Terms)* — The power to position insurance where an agent or broker sees fit. This power is granted by the policy owner.

Control provision *(Life Insurance)* — A condition that states that control is to be given to someone other than the insured. Usually found in contracts for underage people.

Controlled business — The amount of insurance sold by an insurance provider to family and friends. In some states, a limit is placed on this type of business.

C

Controlled insurance *(General Insurance Terms)* — Insurance that is controlled by agent or broker influence, instead of by an agreement.

Convention blank *(General Insurance Terms)* — A financial statement required in every state. This statement is filed each year in the insurance company's home state as well as any other state where the insurer possesses a license.

Convention values *(General Insurance Terms)* — The values attributed to the insurer's assets in the convention blank. *See convention blank.*

Conversion *(General Insurance Term/Health Insurance/Life Insurance)* — In life insurance or health insurance, a transfer from one form of insurance policy to another. In general, a term for the unauthorized use of property that is lawfully in someone's possession.

Conversion fund *(Pensions)* — A fund that supplements a life insurance or limited payment life. The fund increases the amount of cash dispersed at the time of retirement, thereby providing the insured with a monthly income.

Conversion privilege *(Health Insurance/Life Insurance)* — The insured's ability to change from a group to individual policy, should he or she leave the group.

Convertible *(Life Insurance)* — Refers to an insurance policy with a provision that stipulates the policy can be converted to another type of policy.

Convertible collision insurance *(Vehicle Insurance)* — A policy that covers all losses after claims exceeding the deductible have been paid. This type of policy is rare.

Cooperative insurance *(General Insurance Terms)* — A policy issued by an association; for example, a trade union.

Coordination of benefits *(Health Insurance/Life Insurance)* — A stipulation in a group policy that assists in determining which insurer is the primary, shuld the insured be covered by more than one insurer.

Co-pay *(Health Insurance)* — Comparable to coinsurance. The insured pays a portion of the cost for services and the provider pays the rest.

Co-pay provision *(Health Insurance)* — A provision stating what portion of a claim the insurer will pay and what portion will be paid by the insured.

Corridor *(Life Insurance)* — A concept in universal life insurance. The corridor is the amount of pure insurance protection above the accumulation value to qualify as life insurance for tax purposes.

Corridor deductible *(Health Insurance)* — A medical stipulation that makes a deductible, called a corridor, available. The corridor exists after payment of hospital and medical costs up to a certain amount, and before more expenses are shared through coinsurance.

Cost contract *(Health Insurance)* — A contract between a health care provider and the Health Care Financing Administra-

C

tion. The provider agrees to provide services to people covered under the plan at a reasonable cost.

Cost of insurance *(Life Insurance)* — A way of determining the net cost of life insurance to the insured. The total amount the insured gets back from the insurer is deducted from the total amount the insured has paid to the insurer.

Cost of insurance charge *(Life Insurance)* — Synonym for the mortality charge. The charge associated with the pure insurance protection element of a life insurance policy.

Cost of living benefit *(Health Insurance)* — A disability benefit in which the benefit is increased after 12 months and annually thereafter.

Cost of living rider *(Life Insurance)* — A rider that provides for an increase in benefits due to changes in cost of living. Increases are usually done because of changes in the Consumer Price Index.

Cost sharing *(Health Insurance)* — A system wherein the people covered pay a fraction of health care costs, for example, co-payments.

Countersignature *(General Insurance Terms)* — A licensed insurance agent or representative's signature on a policy.

Countersignature law *(Legal Terminology)* — The state law mandating a signature by the representative of the insurer on any insurance contract in that state.

Countrywide rates *(General Insurance Terms)* — A listing of rates and minimum premiums for each major division in the Commercial Lines Manual.

Countrywide rules *(General Insurance Terms)* — A listing of rules and rating factors for each major division in the Commercial Lines Manual.

Coupon policy *(Life Insurance)* — A policy with coupons for a particular sum attached. The insured may turn these in each year when he or she pays the annual premium.

Cover *(General Insurance Terms)* — An insurance contract. This term can also be used to describe the act of incorporating something in a contract of insurance, for example, a newly acquired vehicle. It can also mean to provide coverage to an insured person.

Cover note *(General Insurance Terms)* — A note written by an agent notifying the insured that his or her coverage has taken effect. Comparable to a binder, but not issued by a company like a binder.

Coverage *(General Insurance Terms)* — The extent of the insurance benefit supplied by the insurance contract.

Coverage part *(General Insurance Terms)* — Any of the parts of commercial coverage that may be included with a commercial contract. These may be issued as a policy or attached to part of a policy.

Coverage trigger *(Liability)* — A means for determining if a policy covers a claim.

Covered expenses *(Health Insurance)* — Expenses that qualify for reimbursement or coverage under a policy.

C

Covered loss *(General Insurance Terms)* — Any type of loss the insurer will pay for under a policy. This can include death, injury, property damage or loss, or automobile collision.

Covered person *(General Insurance Terms)* — Any person covered under an insurance contract.

Crash coverage *(Aviation Insurance)* — Insurance that covers damage to an airplane due to a crash. This type of coverage is optional in an aviation policy.

Credentialing *(Health Insurance)* — The process of endorsing a health care provider to participate in or provide care under a health care plan.

Credit carried forward *(Reinsurance)* — Under a spread loss or another form of long-term reinsurance, "credit carried forward" refers to the process of transferring credit or profit from one accounting period to another.

Credit card insurance *(Property Insurance)* — Coverage usually provided under a homeowner's policy that covers the insured in the event of fraudulent credit card use.

Credit health insurance *(Health Insurance)* — Group insurance that covers a creditor against debtors in the event of a total disability. This is a form of disability income insurance.

Credit insurance *(Health Insurance/Life Insurance)* — Insurance that will pay the insured's debts, should he or she die or become disabled.

Credit life insurance *(Life Insurance)* — A group contract that shields a creditor in case the insured dies before paying his or her debt in full.

Crime *(Legal Terminology)* — An act that is forbidden by criminal law. Crimes are considered a public wrong, as opposed to torts, which are private wrongs. Crimes are covered under certain types of policies; for example, commercial crime coverage.

Criticism *(General Insurance Terms)* — An auditor's submission of a modification to an insurer.

Cromie rule *(Property Insurance)* — A technique for apportioning loss under policies with nonidentical coverage.

Crop insurance *(Property Insurance)* — Covers loss of crops due to weather conditions, for example, rain or hail.

Cross purchase *(Life Insurance)* — A type of business life insurance in which both parties in a buyout agreement insure each other.

Cross purchase agreement *(Pensions)* — A contract in which each partner agrees to buy out the interest of a deceased or permanently disabled partner. This type of agreement is usually used with partnerships.

Cumulative liability *(Reinsurance)* — The total liability a reinsurer has accumulated from different policies taken on from different ceding companies that were all affected by the same disaster.

Currently insured status *(General Insurance Terms)* — Under Old Age, Survivors, and Disability Health Insurance, this is a status with less requirements to obtain than a status of fully insured. This status also allows the insured's dependents to survivor benefits in the case of the insured's death.

Custodial care *(Health Insurance)* — Assistance with personal care, for example, eating, bathing, and dressing. This type of care must be given per doctors orders, but does not require that a medical professional be the one providing the care.

Custodian *(Criminal)* — In commercial crime coverage, the custodian is the person who has custody or takes care of any property on the insured's premises.

Customary charge *(Health Insurance)* — The average cost of a certain medical procedure in a particular area during the previous year. This amount is used for establishing Medicare benefits.

Customized coverage *(Health Insurance)* — Coverage tailored to the individual's specific needs, comprised of different policy types.

Cut off *(Reinsurance)* — A stipulation in a reinsurance contract, which states that the reinsurer will not be held liable for losses caused by events that occur after the termination date.

D

D ratio *(Workers Compensation)* — The ratio of losses less than $2,000 combined with the discounted value of larger losses, as compared to total losses expected of an insured in a certain kind of business. This ratio is used to compile workers compensation experience ratings.

Daily report *(General Insurance Terms)* — A condensed statement containing relevant policy information sent to the insurer, the agent, and select others. This is usually the top page of the policy.

Damages *(Legal Terminology)* — The total monetary amount needed to compensate for a loss.

Data processing coverage *(Property Insurance)* — A form of coverage that protects the insured against a data processing system failure. The insured is also covered for the cost of restoring the system.

Date of issue *(General Insurance Terms)* — The date the policy was created by the insurer. This can be a different date than the effective date.

Date of service *(Health Insurance)* — The date the insured was seen by a health care practitioner or given medical treatment.

Death benefit *(Life Insurance)* — The total amount payable to the beneficiary upon the death of the insured, as stated in the policy.

Death benefit only plan *(Life Insurance/Pensions)* — A plan wherein a portion of the insured's salary is collected, to be paid out in case of the insured's death.

Debit *(General Insurance Terms)* — The amount of premiums outstanding and business to be collected by debit or home service agents. This can also refer to the area these customers live in.

Debit system *(Life Insurance)* — A system used by agents to collect policy premiums weekly or monthly.

Debris removal clause *(Property)* — In a property insurance contract, this clause allows the insured to be reimbursed for expenses associated with cleanup of debris created by an insured loss.

Decedent *(General Insurance Terms)* — Synonym for deceased.

Declaration *(Legal Terminology/Liability/Property Insurance)* — A legal term for a written declaration, made under oath, of what the individual knows to be factual information. In liability or property insurance, a declaration is the part of the contract that contains basic information, for example, the insured's contact information or the address of the property.

Declination *(General Insurance Terms)* — When the insurer declines an application for coverage.

Decreasing term *(Life Insurance)* — Coverage with a death benefit that declines to a zero balance throughout the term.

Decreasing term insurance *(Life Insurance)* — A term life insurance policy where the premium stays the same but the death benefit decreases.

Deductible *(General Insurance Terms)* — A fraction of the insured loss that must be paid by the insured before the insurer will pay.

Deductible carryover credit *(Health Insurance)* — Charges accumulated from October to December that are applied toward the next year's deductible, regardless of whether the previous year's deductible was met.

Deductible clause *(General Insurance Terms)* — A clause in the contract that states the deductible amount.

Deep pockets liability *(Legal Terminology)* — Another term for a legal concept known as joint-and-several liability. This states that damages can be obtained from co-defendants based on who is capable of paying, rather than who was found to be more negligent.

Defamation *(Legal Terminology/General Insurance Terms)* — A legal term for a statement meant to damage a person's reputation or business. In insurance law, defamation refers to a deceitful trade practice meant to harm a person working in the insurance business. This is done through untrue, deprecating statements.

Defendant *(Legal Terminology)* — The person being sued in a lawsuit or other court action.

Deferred annuity *(Annuity)* — An annuity in which payments are designated to begin at a later date, as opposed to one where payments begin upon purchase. *See Annuity.*

Deferred compensation *(Pensions)* — A qualified or non-qualified plan wherein a key employee is able to defer current payments until death, disability, or retirement. This must be agreed upon with the employer in a written statement.

Deferred compensation plan *(Pensions)* — Deferment of a fraction of an executive's salary to supplement retirement income. The employer and employee must write an agreement stating the length of the deferral period, per the IRS. This plan is used to encourage employee loyalty.

Deferred group annuity *(Annuity)* — A group annuity contract that allows for the annual purchase of a paid-up, deferred annuity for each one in the group. The total of the annuity payments usually begins at retirement.

Deferred premium *(Life Insurance)* — Premiums on a life insurance policy that have yet to be paid and are not yet due.

Deferred vesting *(Life Insurance)* — A type of vesting wherein rights to the benefits are attained by the member once they have satisfied certain requirements. *See Vesting.*

Deficiency reserve *(Life Insurance)* — A secondary reserve. If the premium charged on a group of insureds is less than the net premium reserve or modified reserve, this reserve must be shown on the balance sheet.

Defined benefit pension plan *(Pensions)* — A retirement plan wherein an employer makes contributions for each employee to supply them with a particular benefit. The total benefit is expressly stated but the amount of each contribution is not.

Defined contribution pension plan *(Pensions)* — A pension plan wherein contributions are predetermined, either as a flat amount or as a percentage of the employees pay. The benefit amount is the total of the contributions.

Degree of care *(Legal Terminology)* — The degree of care taken for the physical safety of others.

Degree of risk *(General Insurance Terms)* — A concept similar to probability. The uncertainty present in a particular situation. The chance that the reality will be different than the predicted outcome.

Delay clause *(Life Insurance)* — A clause that prohibits liability due to damages or loss due to delayed travel.

Delayed payment clause *(Life Insurance)* — A clause within life insurance, stating that payout of benefits to the beneficiary will be delayed for a set amount of time after the insured's death. If the primary beneficiary is deceased at the end of this time period, the benefits will be paid to contingent beneficiaries or the deceased's estate. This clause is often used in the case of a common disaster where the insured and the beneficiary are both killed.

Delivered business *(Life Insurance)* — Contracts delivered to the insured that have not yet been paid for.

Delivery *(Health Insurance/Life Insurance)* — The delivery of a life or health policy to the insured's physical possession.

Demolition clause *(Property Insurance)* — A clause that prohibits liability for costs incurred by demolishing property that is not damaged. This is frequently done due to building ordinances that require demolition of structures after they suffer a certain amount of damage.

Demolition insurance *(Property Insurance)* — Insurance that covers the charges stemming from or for demolition that are not covered under a demolition clause. This can also refer to insurance that covers the cost of demolition in case of a peril that causes the building to require demolition; for example, a fire.

Demurrer *(Legal Terminology)* — A statement in a court case avowing that there is no grounds for action, even if the other party's claims are accurate.

Dental insurance *(Health Insurance)* — A group contract that pays for selected dental services.

Dental plan *(Health Insurance)* — Any contract for dental care, whether supplied on a prepaid basis or paid for afterward, whether group or individual.

Dental plan organization *(Health Insurance)* — A provider of dental care to people or groups. The DPO may be an agreement for service with providers.

Dependent *(General Insurance Terms)* — A person who is dependent on another person to support him or her and maintain his or her lifestyle.

Dependent care plan *(Health Insurance)* — A benefit to employees wherein the employer reimburses them for child care or provides on-site day care facilities.

Dependent coverage *(Health Insurance/Life Insurance)* — Insurance extended to the spouse and single children of the insured head of a family. Age limits may apply to the children.

Dependent life insurance *(Life Insurance)* — A group life insurance benefit providing death protection to the dependents of an employee covered under the plan.

Dependent properties *(Property Insurance)* — Properties that contribute to the insured's income but are not owned or operated by the insured, for example, customers.

Deposit *(Pensions)* — Payments made toward a fund by the employee, the employer, or both.

Deposit administration *(Liability)* — A group annuity offering an undivided account in which contributions can amass. The money in this account is then used to buy annuities for each person's retirement.

Deposit administration group annuity *(Pensions)* — A group agreement that offers a deposit account before retirement. After retirement, annuities are then purchased from this deposit account.

Deposit or provisional premium *(General Insurance Terms)* — A premium amount derived from an approximate value of the final premium. This premium is paid at the start of the policy.

Deposition *(Legal Terminology)* — A sworn statement taken from a party or witness in a court case. This statement is usually done as an interview, which the person testifying is compelled to attend.

D

Depositor's forgery insurance *(Criminal)* — Insurance that protects the insured against forged or altered financial instruments; for example, checks or promissory notes, made in the insured's name or supposedly signed by the insured.

Depository bond *(Surety)* — A bond promising that government deposits made to a bank will not experience loss.

Depreciation *(General Insurance Terms)* — A loss in the value of property, including car, house, building, or other type of physical items. This loss can be due to wear and tear, usage, or the property becoming outdated.

Depreciation insurance *(Property Insurance)* — Insurance that provides for the replacement value of property that has been damaged. Depreciation is not subtracted from the value of the item.

Designated mental health provider *(Health Insurance)* — The health care provider hired by a medical plan to supply mental health services.

Detoxification *(Health Insurance)* — The physical withdrawal from alcohol or drugs experienced by an individual, usually while under medical supervision.

Deviated rate *(General Insurance Terms)* — A rate, offered by a company that usually follows the rates recommended by a lawyer, which is lower than the recommended rate in that area.

Deviation *(General Insurance Terms)* — A rate that is different from the manual rate.

Devise *(Estate)* — Real estate given as a gift through a legal last will.

Diagnosis *(Health Insurance)* — Identifying a disease through testing and medical attention.

Diagnosis related groups *(Health Insurance)* — A way of establishing how to compensate medical providers for their services.

Difference in conditions *(Property Insurance)* — A contract separate from the existing policy that complements or increases the property insurance, so that the property is now protected from all risks, minus some exclusions.

Direct loss *(Property Insurance)* — Damage that directly occurs as a result of a particular hazard. For example, flood damage.

Direct selling system *(General Insurance Terms)* — A system for selling insurance wherein the insurer sells directly to the insured via its employees. This includes insurance sold through mail order services.

Direct writer *(Liability/Property Insurance)* — An insurer who sells his or her products through the direct selling system, or the exclusive agency system.

Direct written premium *(Liability/Property Insurance)* — The amount of the premiums that have been collected, before deducting any premiums sent to reinsurers.

Directed verdict *(Legal Terminology)* — A verdict awarded to the defendant in a court case, based on the plaintiff's failure to prove his or her case.

Director of insurance *(General Insurance Terms)* — A term used for the leader of the department of insurance in some states.

Directors and officers liability insurance *(Liability)* — Insurance that covers officers and directors of an organization from liability claims stemming from their suspected misjudgments and unjust acts.

Disability *(General Insurance Terms)* — A medical condition or psychological affliction that limits the individual's capability to engage in everyday activities. This may be a temporary or permanent circumstance.

Disability benefit *(Health Insurance/Life Insurance)* — A benefit paid to the insured upon being deemed partially or totally disabled. This benefit may be paid out from a disability policy or a clause of a life insurance policy.

Disability benefits law *(Health Insurance)* — A law currently in effect in some states, including California, New York, Hawaii, and Rhode Island. The law mandates disability benefits be paid to workers by the employer for injuries that take place outside the workplace.

Disability buy sell *(Health Insurance)* — A type of income policy that funds a disability buy sell agreement to buy the interests of a disabled stockholder. *See buy sell agreement.*

Disability income insurance *(Health Insurance)* — Insurance that covers the insured in the event that he or she is sick or injured to the point of not being able to work. Under this type of policy, payments are made at regular intervals to replace a regular income.

Disability insurance *(Health Insurance/Life Insurance)* — Insurance that pays out in case of a disability that renders the insured unable to earn an income. Policies can provide coverage in the case of total, catastrophic, or residual disability.

Disability Insurance Training Council Inc. *(Health Insurance)* — A branch of the National Association of Health Underwriters that attempts to support education by local health associations. The council also administers university and executive seminars.

Disability insured *(Health Insurance)* — A status that the insured must be granted by the Social Security Administration to collect disability benefits. This status is only granted if the insured has paid social security taxes in 20 of the 40 quarters preceding the claim being filed.

Disability pension *(Life Insurance)* — A pension paid out to a worker who has become disabled. This is usually paid at a normal retirement age.

Disappearing deductible *(Property Insurance)* — A deductible that progressively fades away as the loss amount grows bigger. A deductible of $50 to $500 is progressively reduced, and losses that equal $500 are fully covered.

Discharge planning *(Health Insurance)* — Conceiving a plan to treat the patient's medical requirements after he or she is released from inpatient treatment.

Disclosure authorization form *(General Insurance Terms)* — A form that permits the disclosure of private information acquired during an insurance-related business. By law, the form must disclose what information will be collected and who it will be shared with.

Discount *(Pensions)* — The difference between the amount that will be due at a specific date in the future and the present value, calculated at a specific rate of interest.

Discounted value table *(General Insurance Terms)* — A table that gives the value of dollars payable at certain times in the future. The table shows values at present and discounted, for different interest rates.

Discovery cover *(Reinsurance)* — A treaty that covers losses found during the term of the treaty, no matter when the loss actually occurred. *See Treaty reinsurance.*

Discovery period *(Surety)* — A grace period given to an insured who has cancelled a bond, during which he or she can still discover and report losses that occurred during the bond's term. Losses reported in this fashion are paid by the original surety. The grace period is usually one year.

Discrimination *(General Insurance Terms)* — Prohibited by law, discrimination is the refusal to insure certain people who have the same characteristics as others who have been insured.

Dishonesty, disappearance, and destruction policy *(Criminal)* — Once called the 3-D policy, this was a common form of commercial crime protection, used to protect the insured against losses caused by employee fraud and forgery, among other causes.

Dismemberment *(Health Insurance)* — The loss of particular parts of the body, or the use of them, due to accidental injury.

Dismemberment benefit *(Health Insurance)* — Benefits paid out upon dismemberment of the insured.

Divided cover *(General Insurance Terms)* — Insuring a person or object with more than one insurer.

Dividend *(General Insurance Terms)* — When an insurer returns part of the premium paid by an insured for a policy, or a part of a surplus paid to each stockholder in a company.

Dividend accumulation *(Life Insurance)* — An option in a life insurance policy that allows the insured to accumulate any dividends paid out to him or her. These dividends stay with the insurer and earn compound interest.

Dividend additions *(Life Insurance)* — An option in a policy that allows the insured to leave the dividends paid out to him or her by the insurer with the insurer. These dividends are then used to purchase a single premium life insurance policy.

Dividend option *(Life Insurance)* — Under certain life insurance policies, an option that allows the insured to choose an alternate way to collect dividends.

Divisible contract clause *(Property Insurance)* — A clause stating that coverage will not be voided at all locations if the conditions of the policy are violated at another location.

Dollar limit *(Property Insurance)* — A limit on coverage in a homeowners policy. This is usually listed in the Coverage C section of the policy.

Domestic insurer *(General Insurance Terms)* — An insurance company founded in the same state that it operates in.

Double indemnity *(Health Insurance/Life Insurance)* — In the case of an accidental death or other specific cases, twice the policy's value may be paid out.

Double protection *(Life Insurance)* — A contract that combines whole life insurance and term life insurance, with the future expiration date of the term policy stated. If the insured should die before the expiration date of the term life policy, both policies will pay out.

Dram shop laws *(Legal Terminology)* — A liability law that applies to serving alcohol or otherwise contributing to another person's intoxication. Any person engaged in either activity could be found liable for the injuries sustained by the intoxicated person, or the damages they cause.

Dram shop liability insurance *(Liability)* — Insurance that covers the proprietors of a business that serves alcohol. The insurance protects them from being liable for accidents caused by customers who became intoxicated inside the establishment.

Dread disease policy *(Health Insurance)* — Insurance that covers all medical costs associated with treating the medical conditions listed in the policy.

Drive other car endorsement *(Vehicle Insurance)* — An extra form of coverage that may be tacked on to an automobile insurance policy. The endorsement covers the policyholder while driving cars that he or she does not own.

Drug formulary *(Health Insurance)* — A list of approved prescription medications that the plan will cover and that will be distributed from affiliated pharmacies.

Drug price review *(Health Insurance)* — A process wherein the American Druggist Blue Book is used to establish the wholesale cost of medication. This information is then used to settle on a maximum drug price.

Drug utilization review *(Health Insurance)* — A process of appraising and reconsidering the usage of drugs to determine the effectiveness of drug treatment.

Druggists' liability insurance *(Liability)* — Insurance that covers a druggist against liability stemming from filling prescriptions, unfulfilled drug deliveries, and the like.

Dual choice *(Health Insurance)* — A federal regulation which states that certain employers must offer an indemnity plan and an HMO. This applies to employers who have a minimum of 25 employees, who are paying minimum wage or more, who offer health care coverage, and who have a federally certified HMO in the area.

Dual life stock company *(General Insurance Terms)* — A type of life insurance company that issues participating and nonparticipating policy contracts.

Dun & Bradstreet, Inc. *(General Insurance Terms)* — A company that aids insurers in underwriting possible insureds by providing the insurer with financial information.

Duplicate coverage inquiry *(Health Insurance)* — An inquiry into the existing coverage on a potential policyholder. This is done to coordinate benefit stipulations if more than one company is involved.

Duplication of benefits *(Health Insurance)* — When similar or indistinguishable coverage exists between two or more insurers.

Dwelling forms *(Property Insurance)* — A type of form that someone fills out; it describes a policy that covers a building in which people reside and the personal possessions kept within.

Earned income *(General Insurance Terms)* — The money a person earns from working at a job.

Earned premium *(General Insurance Terms)* — The portion of a premium exhausted during the policy's term.

Earnings insurance *(Property Insurance)* — Business interruption insurance without a coinsurance clause. This coverage is meant for smaller risks.

Earth movement *(Property Insurance)* — A danger often excluded from homeowners policies; for example, an earthquake, mudslide, or the sinking of the earth. Earth movement is also often excluded from commercial property policies.

Earthquake insurance *(Property Insurance)* — Insurance that covers loss of property or damage due to an earthquake.

Easement *(Property Insurance)* — A right to make use of land belonging to another person.

E

Economic risk *(Pensions)* — A risk to securities investors caused by the lack of predictability of the economy.

Educational assistance plan *(Pensions)* — A benefit offered by the employer, wherein the employee's educational costs are repaid.

Educational fund *(Liability)* — A fund that supplies money for a child's education if the family's breadwinner dies. Part of a life insurance policy.

Effective date *(General Insurance Terms)* — The date an insurance policy takes effect.

Elective benefits *(Health Insurance)* — A lump sum payment for specific injuries; for example, dislocations. These can be chosen instead of payment in installments.

Elective deferral plan *(Pensions)* — A plan wherein policyholders are able to defer present payments into a retirement plan.

Electrical or electrical apparatus exemption clause *(Property Insurance)* — A clause that provides that damage to appliances stemming from electrical currents is only covered if a fire begins.

Electronic data processing coverage *(Property Insurance)* — Insurance that covers computers, data systems, and income lost due to loss of electronic data processing capability.

Elevator collision coverage *(Liability Insurance/Property Insurance)* — Insurance that covers damage to elevators brought about by elevator collision. This insurance also covers personal possessions and the building that houses the elevator. This coverage is often included in business liability insurance policies.

Eligibility date *(Health Insurance)* — The date the insured is able to begin receiving benefits.

Eligibility period *(Health Insurance)* — The time frame during which medical costs accumulated will be reimbursed by a medical policy. This term can also mean the time frame during which prospective insureds can enroll in a group life program or health program without having to prove their insurability.

Eligibility requirements *(Health Insurance/Life Insurance)* — Conditions that must be met before being deemed eligible for coverage under group insurance or pension plan.

Eligible dependent *(Health Insurance)* — A person who depends on the policyholder for financial support, who is deemed eligible for benefits under the policy contract.

Eligible employee *(Health Insurance)* — An employee who is eligible for benefits under the group policy contract.

Eligible expenses *(Health Insurance)* — Medical costs or other charges deemed under the health plan contract as being eligible for coverage.

Eligible person *(Health Insurance)* — A person deemed eligible for coverage under the contract. Unlike an eligible employee, this person does not necessarily work for a certain employer. They may be union members or part of an association.

Elimination period *(Health Insurance)* — The waiting or probation period in a health insurance policy.

Embezzlement *(Legal Terminology)* — Illegal use of funds or other property trusted to a person's control.

Emergency *(Health Insurance)* — An illness or injury that has a sudden onset and needs immediate medical attention.

Emergency accident benefit *(Health Insurance)* — A benefit under a group medical policy that compensates the policyholder for emergency medical attention sought for accidents.

Emergency fund *(Life Insurance)* — A life insurance policy benefit that provides funds to the deceased's survivors for emergency costs, in the time period before his or her estate is finalized.

Employee benefit program *(Health Insurance/Life Insurance)* — Benefits provided to an employee by the employer for expenses such as medical care, death, or disability.

Employee certificate of insurance *(Health Insurance/Life Insurance)* — The proof of membership in a group plan given to an employee. This usually consists of a short outline of the plan's benefits and a certificate of insurance.

Employee contribution *(Health Insurance/Pension)* — In health insurance, the portion of premium expenses paid by the employee. In pensions, a pay deduction applied to a retirement plan.

Employee dishonesty *(Criminal)* — Any false act by an employee that causes a loss to the employer.

Employee dishonesty coverage form *(Criminal)* — Insurance that covers the loss of money and other property that is caused by an employee's dishonesty. This is actually a commercial crime policy in the form of a fidelity bond.

Employee pension benefit plan *(Pensions)* — An employer-created-and-maintained program that offers retirement benefits or defers income until the employee is terminated.

Employee Retirement Income Security Act *(Life Insurance)* — An act outlining federal criteria concerning pension plans, including participation requirements, financial responsibility, and financing.

Employee stock ownership plan *(Pensions)* — An employee plan under which qualified employees are offered part ownership in the company they are employed by. Under this type of plan, stock certificates are produced and maintained in trust for the employee.

Employee welfare benefit plan *(Pensions)* — Any employer-maintained plan, offering policyholders and their dependents services or benefits upon illness, death, or unemployment. These may include medical care or other benefits.

Employees trust *(Pensions)* — A way to finance pensions or profit sharing.

Employer contribution *(Health Insurance)* — The fraction of a plan's cost paid by the employer.

Employer's liability coverage *(Workers Compensation)* — Coverage against the employer's common law liability for injuries to an employee, separate from the employer's liability under workers compensation law. This is known as coverage part B under standard workers compensation policies.

Employer's non-ownership liability insurance *(Annuity)* — Insurance that covers the employer from liability stemming from the employee using his or her car for employer business.

Employment benefit plan *(Pensions)* — A plan comprising a pension plan and a welfare plan for employees.

Encounter *(Health Insurance)* — A meeting with a health care provider, in which the insured receives any type of service.

Encumbrance *(Legal Terminology)* — A claim to a property that reduces the property owner's interest by its value. This can take the form of a lien or mortgage.

Endorsement *(General Insurance Terms)* — A form that changes the provisions of the contract when attached to the policy.

Endorsement extending period of indemnity *(Property Insurance)* — An attachment to a business interruption policy extending the coverage period to include the time after the business reopens but does not yet do the amount of business it did before the interruption.

Endorsement split dollar *(Liability)* — A plan that gives ownership and control of an employee's life insurance policy to the employer. The employer's endorsement protects the employee's right to policy benefits.

Endowment insurance *(Life Insurance)* — Insurance that states an endowment period, after which time the face value of the policy is paid to the insured if he or she is still living. If the insured dies during the period, the policy is paid to his or her beneficiary.

Enrollee *(Health Insurance)* — A person enrolled in a health insurance plan. This does not include dependents of an insured.

Enrolling unit *(Health Insurance)* — The company or group that has signed up for membership in a health insurance plan.

Enrollment *(Health Insurance)* — The act of signing people up for participation in a health insurance plan. This term may also mean the total number of participants in a health care plan.

Enrollment period *(Health Insurance)* — The time frame during which employees can sign up for participation in a health care plan.

Entire contract clause *(Health Insurance/Life Insurance)* — A contract clause stating that the all pieces of the agreement between insurer and insured are found in the contract. This can include the application, endorsements, and conditions.

Entity agreement *(Life Insurance)* — Usually used with a partnership, an entity agreement is a buy sell arrangement, wherein the partnership promises to buy out the interests of a partner if he or she becomes disabled or dies.

Entry age *(Pensions)* — The age at which an employee can become eligible to participate in a pension plan; usually this is age 65.

Entry date into claims made *(Liability)* — The effective date of a claims made liability policy, which is used to establish the maturity of the policy.

Environmental restoration *(Annuity/Legal Terminology)* — Compensation for destruction of or damage to natural resources by a motor carrier. This can include the cost of minimizing damage to humans, fish, and other wildlife.

Equipment breakdown insurance *(Property Insurance)* — Commercial insurance covering any loss caused by the breakdown of machinery or other equipment.

Equipment floater *(Property Insurance)* — Coverage against specific types of damage on different types of equipment.

Equity *(General Insurance Terms)* — The cash value of an insurer, after liabilities.

Employee Retirement Income Security Act *(ERISA)* **liability** *(Liability)* — A liability that is obligatory for employees who work in a financial capability to ensure the proper handling of pensions and benefits.

Errors and omissions clause *(Reinsurance)* — A clause in a reinsurance treaty that stipulates that errors or omissions made do not nullify the reinsurer's liability.

Errors and omissions insurance *(Liability)* — Insurance that covers the insured against losses incurred due to a mistake on the insured's part. This type of insurance is usually purchased by financial advisors or insurance agents. This can also be a type of insurance that covers a financial institution against failure to obtain adequate insurance coverage.

Estate *(General Insurance Terms)* — All the property a deceased person owns at the time of his or her death.

Estate plan *(General Insurance Terms)* — A will and other provisions for the distribution of one's estate upon death or disability. *See Estate.*

Estate planning *(Estate)* — The administration of an estate, done to minimize estate shrinkage due to taxation.

Estate tax *(Estate)* — A tax based on the worth of the deceased's estate, which is due to the federal government.

Estimated premium *(General Insurance Terms)* — A projected premium amount that is later adjusted.

Estoppel *(Legal Terminology)* — A legal term referring to an individual losing the ability to deny the existence of a condition by virtue of his or her behavior. For example, if a health insurer has paid out several claims to an individual with a certain disease in the past, he or she may be estopped from later claiming the disease is not covered, because the insured was reasonably led to believe it was covered.

Evidence of insurability *(Health Insurance/Life Insurance)* — Any facts about the applicant's health needed to underwrite him or her; for example, a medical physical.

Evidence clause *(General Insurance Terms)* — A clause that obligates the insured to assist the adjuster in determining the legitimacy of a claim by producing documents and being examined. In a health insurance policy, the evidence clause obligates the insured to be physically examined.

Ex gratia payment *(General Insurance Terms)* — Compensation from the insurer that is not required by the contract. The insurer may occasionally pay a claim, although he or she is not liable as an act of goodwill.

Examination *(General Insurance Terms)* — An evaluation conducted by the state insurance department of an insurance company.

Examiner *(General Insurance Terms/Health Insurance/Life Insurance)* — A general term for a state insurance department employee who is sent to audit an insurer. In health insurance or life insurance, an examiner is a doctor assigned by an insurance company to examine prospective policyholders.

Exception *(Health Insurance)* — A clause in the policy contract that voids or removes the obligation for coverage.

Excess insurance *(General Insurance Terms)* — A secondary coverage that pays in excess of the primary policy. Excess insurance does not pay unless the amount lost exceeds a specified amount.

Excess interest *(Liability)* — Interest added to the cash value of a policy above the minimum rate guaranteed by the insurer in the contract.

Excess limit *(Liability)* — A limit provided in a policy that exceeds the basic limit. This term can also mean the limit on a secondary policy that is higher than the first policy limit.

Excess line broker *(General Insurance Terms)* — A broker who has a license to deal with insurers not admitted in his or her state.

Excess loss premium factor *(Workers Compensation)* — A factor compensating the insurer for the insured choosing to limit a large loss using the retrospective rating formula.

Excess of loss reinsurance *(Reinsurance)* — Reinsurance covering the insurance company against losses larger than a certain amount. This term can also refer to reinsurance that covers the ceding company from the part of the loss that comes from a single occurrence that exceeds the first loss, a previously stated amount.

Excess per risk reinsurance *(Reinsurance)* — Reinsurance that covers the ceding company against a loss in excess of a particular retention for each particular occurrence.

Excess plan *(Pensions)* — A plan for retirement funding that takes into account social security.

Exclusion rider *(General Insurance Terms)* — An attachment to a policy that eliminates coverage for certain hazards.

Exclusion *(General Insurance Terms)* — A clause in the contract denying coverage for specific hazards, people, or property.

Exclusive agency system *(General Insurance Terms)* — A system of insurance sales, in which agents only provide business to one company or give the right of first refusal to a certain company.

Exclusive provider organization *(Health Insurance)* — A kind of preferred provider organization in which the insured has a primary care doctor who refers him or her to other providers, instead of the insured having a variety of preferred providers to choose from.

Exhibitions insurance *(Property Insurance)* — Coverage that protects an individual, who displays his or her property at public exhibitions, against damage to the property.

Expectation of life *(Life Insurance)* — The amount of years left in the life of the average person of a certain age, as determined by a mortality table.

Expected claims *(Health Insurance)* — The anticipated amount of claims during a contract year, as determined by statistics.

Expected morbidity *(Health Insurance)* — The anticipated frequency of illness or injury in a particular time frame to a certain group of people, as determined by a mortality table.

Expected mortality *(Life Insurance)* — The anticipated probability of death during a particular time frame to a certain group of people, as determined by a mortality table.

Expediting expenses *(Property Insurance)* — Costs sustained by a business attempting to hurry a reopening after damage.

Expense *(Health Insurance)* — The share of the insurer's operating expenditures, such as underwriting, medical examination costs, salaries, and other expenses that come from each policy.

Expense allowance *(General Insurance Terms)* — Payment made to an insurance agent in addition to set commissions.

Expense constant *(General Insurance Terms)* — A charge added to the premium amount. Most often, this is done to workers compensation policies, or other small policies that have low premiums. The cost of servicing these policies is too much to recoup on premiums alone.

Expense loading *(General Insurance Terms)* — An amount added to the rate to cover expenses.

Expense ratio *(General Insurance Terms)* — The portion of the premium dedicated to paying the insurer's expenses. Losses are not included.

Expense reimbursement allowance *(General Insurance Terms)* — Payment made to an insurance agent in addition to set commissions.

Expense reserve *(General Insurance Terms)* — The liability to the insurer for expenses incurred but not paid.

Expenses *(General Insurance Terms)* — The cost, minus losses, of operating an insurance company.

Experience *(General Insurance Terms)* — The record of loss belonging to an agent, insured, or another category. This term can also mean a statistic made up of the ratio of losses to premiums.

Experience modification *(General Insurance Terms)* — A premium amount increase or decrease caused by the use of an experience rating plan.

Experience rating *(General Insurance Terms)* — A way of adjusting premium amounts based on previous experiences for that specific risk, instead of being based on loss experience for all risks.

Experience refund *(Reinsurance)* — A fixed amount of the net profit of a reinsurance policy that must be given to the ceding insurer under profit sharing at the year's end.

Experienced mortality *(Life Insurance)* — The actual mortality of a given group as opposed to expected mortality.

Experimental procedures *(Health Insurance)* — Any medical service, therapy, or medication that the plan finds to be not yet proven or perceived by the medical community as ineffective.

Expiration *(General Insurance Terms)* — The termination date listed in a contract.

Expiration card *(General Insurance Terms)* — A method of noting the expiration date of a policy. The agent or salesperson may use this to remind him or herself of which policies will be up for renewal soon.

Expiration file *(General Insurance Terms)* — A notation of the day on which policies expire, kept by agents or salespeople.

Expiration notice *(General Insurance Terms)* — Notice given to the insured of upcoming expiration of the insurance.

Expiry *(Life Insurance)* — Ending a term life policy at the end of the coverage period.

Explanation of benefits *(Health Insurance)* — A statement mailed to a policyholder that itemizes services, the amount paid for them, and the amount the patient is liable for.

Explanation of Medicare benefits *(Health Insurance)* — A statement mailed to a Medicare participant explaining the payment of his or her claim.

Explosion collapse and underground damage ("XCU") *(Liability Insurance)* — In business liability insurance, this term is used to denote that these hazards apply to specific kinds of work.

Explosion insurance *(Property Insurance)* — Insurance that covers loss of property because of explosion. This coverage does not apply to explosions of steam boilers and other pressurized instruments.

Exposure *(General Insurance Terms)* — Being in a situation that makes it possible to suffer a loss. This term can also mean the chance of a loss happening due to the area around the insured. Another possible meaning use of this term is in the context of an area around the insured that results in a loss to the insured.

Exposure units *(General Insurance Terms)* — People or possessions that may be subject to a loss that can be given a cash value. This term may also be used to refer to the premium base.

Express authority *(General Insurance Terms)* — Authority granted to the agent by the insurer, by way of the agency agreement.

Extended care facility *(Health Insurance)* — A facility authorized to give 24-hour nursing care under local and state laws; for example, nursing homes.

Extended coverage *(Property Insurance)* — Extends property insurance coverage to protect against more perils, including hail, riot, smoke damage, and windstorm.

Extended death benefit *(Life Insurance)* — A group policy clause that pays out a life insurance benefit if the insured is disabled from the time premiums are no longer paid, until death. This benefit will also be paid if the insured dies within a year of the end of premiums being paid.

E

Extended non-owner liability *(Vehicle Insurance)* — An attachment to an automobile policy that provides coverage for the insured while driving vehicles he or she does not own on a regular basis. It also covers vehicles used to transport people or property for profit and vehicles used for business.

Extended period of indemnity *(Property Insurance)* — Coverage that extends the existing lost income coverage for a certain time frame after business resumes.

Extended reporting period *(Liability Insurance)* — A time frame that allows the insured to make claims after the "claims made" liability coverage has expired.

Extended term insurance *(Life Insurance)* — A clause under many policies that gives the option of continuing the existing insurance for a period based on the contract's cash value.

Extended wait *(Reinsurance)* — A type of reinsurance wherein the reinsurer pays benefits under a disability contract after the ceding company has done so for some months.

Extension of benefits *(Heath Insurance)* — A policy condition that allows employees not currently working, or their hospitalized dependents, to extended coverage past the expiry date of the policy. Extended coverage only lasts until the employee returns to work or the dependent is discharged from the hospital.

Extortion coverage form *(Criminal)* — Commercial crime insurance that covers loss of cash, securities, and other goods as a result of extortion.

Extra expense coverage form *(Property Insurance)* — A form that covers added costs to a business that needs to remain open after a property loss.

Extra expense insurance *(Property Insurance)* — A form that provides compensation for costs associated with the operation of a business damaged by a hazard listed in the insurance contract. This form is usually used by businesses that cannot afford to close for fear of losing customers.

Extra percentage tables *(Health Insurance/Life Insurance)* — A mortality or morbidity table that displays the amount of an extra premium charged for certain medical conditions.

Extra premium *(General Insurance Terms)* — A charge added to a premium because the regular premium rate does not take into account certain hazards.

Extra premium removal *(General Insurance Terms)* — Elimination of an extra premium because the hazard necessitating it no longer exists.

F

Face *(Life Insurance)* — The first page of the policy.

Face amount *(General Insurance Terms)* — The total amount of coverage provided by an insurance contract, as stated on the face.

Facility of payment clause *(Life Insurance)* — A clause in industrial life coverage that states the insurer is permitted to pay some of the policy proceeds to a relative or other person who possesses the policy and seems entitled to the policy. This is done to minimize legal costs when settling an estate.

Facultative reinsurance *(Reinsurance)* — Reinsurance in which the reinsurer has the right to accept or reject each policy presented to him or her by the insurance company.

Fair Credit Reporting Act *(General Insurance Terms)* — A law requiring that applicants for a credit service be forewarned any time a credit report is requested. The applicant must also be given the name and address of the agency reporting any negative information.

Fair Access to Insurance Requirements Plan (FAIR) *(Property Insurance)* — A plan instituted by the federal government, similar to stop loss reinsurance. If a property owner, whether commercial or residential, cannot obtain property insurance, he or she can apply to an insurance agent who works for a FAIR plan insurer. Should the property be found acceptable, he or she will be insured. If not, the company will suggest improvements to the property, and will insure it after the improvements are made.

F

Fair rental value coverage *(Property Insurance)* — Coverage that protects the rental income an insured receives from an insured building. If a building that is usually rented to others is damaged by a hazard named in the policy, this coverage will pay the rental value.

Fallen building clause *(Property Insurance)* — A clause in a property insurance policy stipulating that if a portion of a building collapses for any reason other than fire or explosion, the fire insurance is voided.

Family automobile policy *(Vehicle Insurance)* — A package policy with coverage in case of injury or property damage to another person, the policyholder's injury, and vehicle damage. This type of coverage is mostly nonexistent now, as it has been widely replaced by personal automobile insurance policies.

Family dependent *(Health Insurance)* — An individual who is covered due to being the insured's spouse or single dependent child who resides with the policyholder.

Family expense policy *(Health Insurance)* — An insurance policy that covers all family members' medical costs.

Family income policy *(Life Insurance)* — An insurance policy that provides income until a date in the future. This date is named in the policy after the insured's death. The time frame during which income will be paid is calculated from the policy's inception date. At the end of the income payment period, the total amount of the policy is paid to the policyholder.

Family maintenance policy *(Life Insurance)* — An insurance policy that pays the beneficiary an income from the date of the insured's death for a stated timeframe. When this is over, the face amount of the policy is paid out to the beneficiary.

Family policy *(Life Insurance)* — A policy made up of whole life insurance for the head of a household and term coverage on the rest of the family.

Farm coverage part *(Liability Insurance/ Property Insurance)* — A part offered in the commercial package policy that covers farmland, equipment, and livestock.

Farm liability coverage form *(Liability Insurance)* — A form attached to farm coverage. This form provides bodily injury, property damage, and personal injury coverage.

Farm personal property *(Property Insurance)* — Property not covered under farm property coverage; for example, livestock, grain, and harvest equipment.

Farm property coverage form *(Property Insurance)* — Farm coverage for the residence, household property, and farm buildings.

Farmer's comprehensive personal liability *(Liability Insurance)* — Coverage comparable to comprehensive personal liability but changed to apply to farm perils.

Farmers-ranch owner's policy *(Property Insurance)* — Comparative to homeowners insurance, adapted to cover a farm. Package policy that covers farm residences and the property within, barns, stables, and other farm buildings.

Fire, Casualty, and Surety (FC&S) Bulletins *(General Insurance Terms)* — Bulletins from the National Underwriter Company that detail coverage and underwriting for various types of policies within the categories of insurance.

Federal crime insurance program *(Criminal)* — Program administered by the federal government wherein insurers offer crime insurance for people otherwise unable to get it. Offered on residential and commercial risks in many states.

Federal Deposit Insurance Corporation (FDIC) *(General Insurance Terms)* — A federal government agency that insures bank deposits, up to $250,000.

Federal Employee's Compensation Act *(Workers Compensation)* — Act that mandates workers compensation benefits to civilians working for the federal government. The system is operated by the government, who also offer the benefits, so that no insurers have to be involved.

Federal estate tax *(General Insurance Terms)* — A federal tax on the estate of a deceased person.

Federal Insurance Administration *(General Insurance Terms)* — An division of the U.S. Department of Housing and Urban Development that administers flood plans, FAIR plans, and federal crime insurance.

Federal officials bond *(Surety)* — A bond that compensates the government for losses caused by dishonest employees.

Federal qualification *(Health Insurance)* — Health Care Financing Administration approval of an HMO after a thorough evaluation of their facilities, systems, and business practices.

Fee for service reimbursement *(Health Insurance)* — A system wherein doctors and other health care professionals receive payment based on their charges for services provided.

Fee maximum *(Health Insurance)* — The maximum fee available to a health care professional for a service provided under a contract.

Fee schedule *(Health Insurance)* — A schedule of maximum charges for providers who charge on a fee for service basis.

Fellow servant rule *(Workers Compensation)* — Before workers compensation laws were instituted, the fellow servant rule was used as a defense. This common law principle said that if a worker was hurt because of another worker's negligence, the coworker was to blame instead of the employer.

Federal Insurance Contributions Act (FICA) *(General Insurance Terms)* — A law introduced in 1939 that mandates payroll taxes, which help to fund social security and Medicare benefits. Under FICA, the employer and the employee make equal contributions through their taxes. The employer pays taxes on payroll, while the workers pay taxes on their salaries or wages earned.

Fictitious groups *(General Insurance Terms)* — Fabricated groups created with the intention of purchasing insurance. These groups are barred by law from being insured.

Fiduciary *(General Insurance Terms)* — A person charged with the money or property of another, which is being held in trust. The fiduciary is legally obligated to act ethically in this position.

F

Field *(General Insurance Terms)* — A category of insurance; for example, the health insurance field. This term can also refer to a specific region being served by an agent or insurer.

Field force *(General Insurance Terms)* — The agents and supervisors working for an insurance company in local offices.

Field underwriting *(Health Insurance)* — An initial decision by the insurance agent in the field about a prospective insured, based on whether they may meet the underwriting standards of the insurer.

File and use rating laws *(Legal Terminology)* — State laws that allow insurers to assume new rates without having to seek insurance department approval.

Financed insurance *(Legal Terminology)* — The payment of policy premiums by borrowing against the cash value of the policy.

Financed premium *(Life Insurance)* — Payment of policy premiums with money borrowed from outside of the contract.

Financial responsibility clause *(Vehicle Insurance)* — A clause stipulating that the policy adheres to the laws of the state the vehicle is being operated in.

Financial responsibility law *(Vehicle Insurance)* — A state law requiring the policyholder to prove he or she can pay for losses. Depending on the state, this may be required before any accidents or after the first accident. This evidence is usually an insurance policy.

Fine print *(General Insurance Terms)* — Small-size type in a contract that is purported to contain omissions, exemptions, and coverage limits. State laws largely prohibit printing exclusions in smaller font than that used for the rest of the contract. Laws also mandate the size of font that must be used in contracts.

Fire *(Property Insurance)* — Combustion intense enough to result in a flame or a glow. Only hostile fires, which are unintentional or have grown outside the intended area, are covered by property insurance.

Fire damage limit *(Liability Insurance)* — A limit that only pertains to fire legal liability coverage.

Fire department service clause *(Property Insurance)* — A clause within a fire insurance contract that provides that the insured will be reimbursed for any expenses caused by the fire department attempting to save their property.

Fire legal liability *(Property Insurance)* — A policy that covers the insured in case of liability due to negligence that causes fire to spread to another's property.

Fire maps *(Property Insurance)* — Maps that show all fire insurance written by all insurers. These maps are a visual representation of the insured's covered risks in the area, which helps the insurer to avoid catastrophic losses.

First loss insurance *(General Insurance Terms)* — The first policy that claims are submitted to for a loss, before any other policy that covers the same peril. This term can also mean a policy written for an amount that covers the anticipated loss during the policy term.

First named insured *(General Insurance Terms)* — The first person listed on a commercial insurance policy.

First party insurance *(General Insurance Terms)* — Insurance that covers the policyholder's property or self.

Flat cancellation *(General Insurance Terms)* — A policy cancelled on the effective date. Usually, no premiums have been paid.

Flat commission *(General Insurance Terms)* — A standard commission that is paid to the insurance agent no matter what kind of policy has been sold.

Flat deductible *(Property Insurance)* — A particular sum deducted from every loss or claim filed.

Flat maternity benefit *(Health Insurance)* — A benefit that pays all hospital costs associated with an admission for maternity care, no matter how much the cost of the stay.

Flat rate *(Reinsurance)* — The rate on a reinsurance premium. This rate is derived from the premium income the ceding insurer receives from policies ceded to the reinsurer.

Fleet policy *(Vehicle Insurance)* — A contract for coverage on multiple vehicles, usually five or more.

Flexible benefit plan *(Health Insurance)* — A customizable plan for employee health insurance. Employees can choose benefits to suit their requirements.

Flexible premium policy *(Life Insurance)* — A policy wherein the insured can modify the amount and scheduling of premium payments.

Flexible spending account *(Health Insurance)* — An account made up of funds deducted from an employee's pretax earnings. This account can be used to pay for child care or medical costs not already covered by the plan. Any money left in the account at the year's end is forfeited.

Floater *(Property Insurance)* — Insurance on a movable piece of property, for example, a boat. The insurance is valid regardless of where the property moves, as long as it is within an area established in the contract.

Flood *(Property Insurance)* — A temporary overflow of a normally dry area due to overflow of a body of water, unusual buildup, runoff of surface waters, or abnormal erosion or undermining of shoreline. Floods can also be overflow of mud flow caused by buildup of water underground.

Flood insurance *(Property Insurance)* — Insurance that compensates the insured for the loss of property due to a flood.

Floor plan insurance *(Property Insurance)* — Insurance that covers goods meant for sale that are in the possession of a retailer and have been accepted as collateral for a loan. If the goods are damaged or destroyed, the lender is covered.

Following form *(Property Insurance)* — A form that is written in exactly the same terms as other property insurance policies covering a piece of property.

Foreign insurer *(General Insurance Terms)* — An insurance company housed in a different state than the one the insured's policy is written in.

F

Forfeitures *(Pensions/General Insurance Terms)* — The relinquishing of the right to any future benefits. In pensions, the non-invested funds left over by former employees. These forfeitures must be put toward future employer contributions.

Forgery or alteration coverage form *(Criminal)* — A form of commercial crime insurance that protects against forgery or other modifications made to financial instruments drawn on the insured's accounts.

Form *(General Insurance Terms)* — A document that completes a policy. This term can also mean an endorsement or rider.

Formal plan *(Pensions)* — A retirement plan outlined in writing. Under this plan, legally enforceable rights are passed on to the eligible employees.

Formula *(Pensions)* — An equation used to establish the total pension that will be received or the contribution that will be made from a retirement plan.

Foundation exclusion clause *(Property Insurance)* — A clause found in fire insurance, stating that the value of a property's foundation will not be calculated in the total property value after a loss.

Fractional premium *(General Insurance Terms)* — A premium divided equally and paid at regular intervals, for example, quarterly.

Franchise deductible *(General Insurance Terms)* — A deductible within a policy that states claims under a certain amount or certain percentage of the policy are not covered. Claims that cost more than those amounts are entirely covered.

F

Franchise insurance *(Health Insurance)* — Also called wholesale insurance. A plan for groups that are too small to obtain group coverage. Participants are usually solicited from a workplace with the employer's approval. The plan issues participants with an individual contract with individual underwriting and the same provisions.

Fraternal insurance *(Health Insurance/Life Insurance)* — Insurance written for members of a fraternal group or a lodge.

Fraud *(Legal Terminology)* — Dishonesty and deception with the intent of making a personal gain at the expense of another individual or a company.

Free look *(Health Insurance/Life Insurance)* — A specified time frame during which the insured may scrutinize a recently purchased policy and relinquish the policy if he or she finds it unacceptable. This time frame is often between ten and 30 days.

Free of capture and seizure clause *(Property Insurance)* — A clause stipulating that losses stemming from war, seizure, or takeover are excluded from the policy.

Free of particular average *(General Insurance Terms)* — A clause, usually found in a marine insurance contract, that states losses less than certain amounts are not covered. This is essentially the same as a deductible.

Free standing emergency medical service center *(Health Insurance)* — Sometimes called an urgent care center, this is a facility that provides emergency medical attention.

Free standing outpatient surgical center *(Health Insurance)* — Sometimes called a surgical care center. A facility that provides outpatient services to surgical patients.

Full coverage *(General Insurance Terms)* — Insurance that covers the insured's claim completely.

Full preliminary term reserve valuation *(Life Insurance)* — A life insurance contract that does not make a reserve mandatory within the first year of the contract being established. In the following years, the reserves will be modified to make up for the lack of reserve in the first year.

Full reporting clause *(Property Insurance)* — A clause, most often seen in commercial policies, stipulating that the policyholder must report the property's value to the insured at certain predetermined times. This is done to ensure that coverage is sufficient to cover the value of a potential loss. The policyholder may be assessed a penalty for failing to regularly report the accurate value.

Fully insured status *(General Insurance Terms)* — A clause found within the OASDHI that details the requirements a person must meet to be eligible to collect social security retirement benefits. Most often, the person has to have worked for ten years.

OASDHI stands for "Old Age, Survivors, Disability, and Health Insurance."

Fully paid policy *(Life Insurance)* — A limited payment policy that is fully paid. For example, a 30-pay policy is fully paid after 30 years of regular premium payments.

Funded pension plan *(Pensions)* — Pension plan wherein enough funds are currently available to pay out all future retirement benefit claims.

Funding level *(Health Insurance)* — The amount of money needed to buy a medical care program. Either the premium cost for an insured program or an amount charged for anticipated claim loss and other fees.

Fur and jewelry floater *(Property Insurance)* — Insurance that covers jewelry and furs against all risks, regardless of where they are located.

Future increase option *(Health Insurance)* — An option to augment disability benefits without having to re-establish insurability. This option is available at certain predetermined times listed in the contract.

G

Garage coverage form *(Vehicle Insurance)* — Commercial coverage for businesses with multiple automobiles on their premises, for example, auto repair shops, dealerships, or garages.

Garage keepers' legal liability insurance *(Liability Insurance)* — A form of insurance similar to bailee's insurance. Covers a garage owner against liability for damages done to vehicles in their care or custody.

Garage liability insurance *(Liability Insurance)* — Liability coverage for garage owners or dealerships.

Gatekeeper model *(Health Insurance)* — A type of HMO or PPO wherein the patient's primary care physician acts as a gatekeeper. The gatekeeper is the patient's contact point, and refers the patient for testing and specialist referrals.

Gender rule *(Health Insurance)* — A rule used to establish which parent's policy the children will be covered by. Under this rule, the father's policy will be considered the primary and will pay the claims of dependent children first.

General account *(Annuities)* — The account used to invest the income generated from premiums. Typically, this is an investment portfolio made up of safe, guaranteed investments.

General adjustment bureau *(General Insurance Terms)* — A company that adjusts claims for many different insurers. This is a standalone company that also offers adjuster training.

General agency system *(Life Insurance)* — A system made up of general agents selling life insurance.

General agent *(Health Insurance/Life Insurance)* — A person selected by the insurer to run its business in a specified area. These agents must seek out their own clients and are paid on a commission basis.

General agents and managers conference *(Health Insurance/ Life Insurance)* — A group affiliated with the National Association of Life Underwriters, made up of agents and managers.

General aggregate limit *(Liability Insurance)* — A limit imposed on commercial general liability. This limit can apply to several different types of damages, including those awarded for personal injury, property damage, and bodily injury.

General average *(General Insurance Terms)* — A term usually used in marine insurance to describe a partial loss that was sustained in order to avoid irreparable damage to the entire undertaking.

General liability insurance *(Liability Insurance)* — Insurance for business owners that covers against liability caused by various perils. Coverage usually includes bodily injury incurred on the insured's property, or losses due to a product sold by the insured.

General power of appointment *(Estate)* — The power of the recipient of a property interest to pass it on to another person of their choosing.

General property form *(Property Insurance)* — A widely used form of commercial insurance, used to protect the property from risks specified in the contract.

Generation skipping transfer *(Estate)* — A gift or inheritance of property received by a person two generations or more below the owner.

Geographical limitation *(General Insurance Terms)* — A clause that lists the only geographic areas in which coverage is effective.

Glass coverage form *(Property Insurance)* — A form that covers commercial glass; for example, plate glass.

Good driver discount *(Vehicle Insurance)* — A discount given to drivers who qualify as good drivers under certain criteria; for example, amount of tickets issued to the driver or the length of time the driver has had the license.

Governing classification *(Workers Compensation)* — The classification given to a company based on the highest amount of payroll.

Grace period *(Health Insurance/Life Insurance)* — A time period during which payment must be made and the policy is in effect.

Graded commission *(General Insurance Terms)* — A schedule of commissions payable to agents. The commission amount varies based on the category or amount of the policies written.

Graded death benefits *(Life Insurance)* — Most commonly seen in life insurance policies written for children; this type of death benefit increases over time. At first, the amount of the benefit paid out may be less than the policy's face amount.

G

Graded premium *(Life Insurance)* — A premium that is a lower amount in the beginning of the contract and increases.

Grading schedule for cities and towns *(Property Insurance)* — A schedule that is used to determine a given city's fire rating. The fire rating is determined by multiple factors. The schedule is created by the National Board of Fire Underwriters.

Graduated life table *(Life Insurance)* — A mortality table that has had a formula applied to it.

Grantee *(General Insurance Terms)* — In real estate, a term used for the person buying.

Grantor *(General Insurance Terms)* — In real estate, a term used for the person selling.

Grievance procedure *(Health Insurance)* — A process instituted by a health plan or benefit provider for policyholders to file complaints.

Gross earnings *(Property Insurance)* — An amount calculated by deducting the cost of goods sold from the total sales.

Gross earnings form *(Property Insurance)* — A form that is no longer widely used. This form was used in writing business interruption coverage.

Gross line *(General Insurance Terms)* — The maximum amount an insurer will insure on a particular risk.

Gross negligence *(Legal Terminology)* — Negligence that is found to be intentional.

Gross premium *(General Insurance Terms/Life Insurance)* — A general term for an amount made up of the net premium plus expenses and commissions. In life insurance, the premium assessed for life insurance.

Ground coverage *(Aviation Insurance)* — Insurance for risks to the airplane body while not flying. Perils are specified as either "not in flight" or "not in motion." "Not in flight" coverage also covers the aircraft during taxi.

Group *(Health Insurance)* — Many people covered under a contract together. Most often, a group is comprised of employees of a particular business.

Group annuity *(Annuities)* — An annuity that funds a retirement plan for a group. The annuity contract is written on a group basis. The group itself is usually made up of employees of the same employer.

Group certificate *(Health Insurance/Life Insurance)* — A certificate given to each policyholder of a group plan. The certificate lists the benefits offered under the group policy.

Group contract *(Health Insurance/Life Insurance)* — A contract for insurance that is made with a group of people, usually employees of the same employer.

Group credit insurance *(Health Insurance/Life Insurance)* — Insurance that covers the life or well-being of a debtor. This type of insurance pays or reduces the debt should the debtor become disabled or die.

Group disability insurance *(Health Insurance)* — Group policy providing coverage for reduced income due to disability or illness.

Group health insurance *(Health Insurance)* — Group coverage that provides the group members with benefits for hospital stays, medical examinations, treatment, and doctors' fees. These plans usually contain mandatory deductibles and coinsurance payments.

Group I rates *(Property Insurance)* — Term used in place of "Fire Rates" under the newest commercial lines program. Rates in Group I include those for fire, explosion, and vandalism.

Group II rates *(Property Insurance)* — Term used in place of "Extended Coverage Rates" under the newest commercial lines program. Rates in Group II include those for hail, riots, and vehicles.

Group life insurance *(Life Insurance)* — Life insurance coverage provided to a group of people, most often employees of the same company. These policies carry a lower cost than the policies offered to individuals, due to the tax cuts offered to the insurer, the use of adverse selection, and the sharing of expenses.

Group model HMO *(Health Insurance)* — An HMO that contracts with certain provider groups, with whom rates for medical care are negotiated. The HMO then pays the negotiated rate for care provided to the policyholders. Contracts are also made with hospitals for care provided to the policyholders.

Group ordinary life insurance *(Pensions)* — Life insurance with an equal premium issued to groups.

Group permanent insurance *(Pensions)* — A plan issued to groups that blends retirement benefits with life insurance. This type of plan uses an equal premium.

Group permanent life insurance *(Life Insurance)* — A form of group life insurance wherein the policyholders are offered one of many plans of permanent life insurance.

Group property and liability insurance *(Liability Insurance/ Property Insurance)* — A policy providing liability and property insurance in a fashion similar to a group life insurance policy.

Group renewable term insurance *(Pensions)* — A group life insurance policy that only covers a certain pre-defined period of time, usually a year. This type of policy is renewable at the end of the policy's term.

Group retirement income insurance *(Pensions)* — Group insurance policy with an equal premium throughout the policy, which provides a retirement income.

Guaranteed cash value *(Life Insurance)* — A term for a concept in whole life insurance. Under a whole life insurance policy, the cash value of the policy increases over the policy's term until the insured reaches the age of 100. At this age, the cash value of the policy will be equal to the face amount of the policy.

Guaranteed cost premium *(Liability Insurance/Worker's Compensation)* — A premium based on another factor besides loss experience, for example, a certain specified rating. The cost is guaranteed because it will never be adjusted on the basis of the insured's loss experience during the policy's term.

Guaranteed insurability *(Health Insurance/Life Insurance)* — A contract option stating that the insured may purchase extra insurance in specified increments at specified times without having to prove insurability again.

Guaranteed renewable *(Health Insurance/Life Insurance)* — A contract the insurer must renew without changing any part of, except for the premium rate. The insured has the opportunity to renew this contract at a specified point in time or a specified age.

Guaranteed standard issue *(Health Insurance)* — A term used for a group plan that covers all policyholders no matter what their medical history may contain.

Guaranty funds *(General Insurance Terms)* — A fund mandated by state law. The fund is comprised of money from the insurers currently conducting business in that state, which is available to companies unable to cover debts or unpaid claims. These are sometimes called Insolvency Funds.

Guertin laws *(Liability Insurance)* — Laws on nonforfeiture and valuation, made standard in 1947. The name is derived from then head of the NAIC committee responsible for developing these laws, Alfred Guertin.

Guest law *(Legal Terminology)* — A law that limits the rights of a passenger in an automobile to demand funds from the driver on the basis of negligence. Typically, the passenger must prove willful and wanton negligence by the driver before they can collect any funds.

Guest property coverage *(Criminal)* — Commercial coverage form for the property of hotel or motel guests. Two forms exist: One covers property placed inside a safe deposit box on the premises, and the other covers the legal liability of the company for losses incurred on their premises or damages done to property while in the insured's possession.

Guideline premium *(Life Insurance)* — The highest premium permitted by the IRS under a policy classified as a life insurance policy.

Guiding principles *(General Insurance Terms)* — Principles that guide sharing the coverage of a loss between two insurance companies. These principles are developed by property and liability associations.

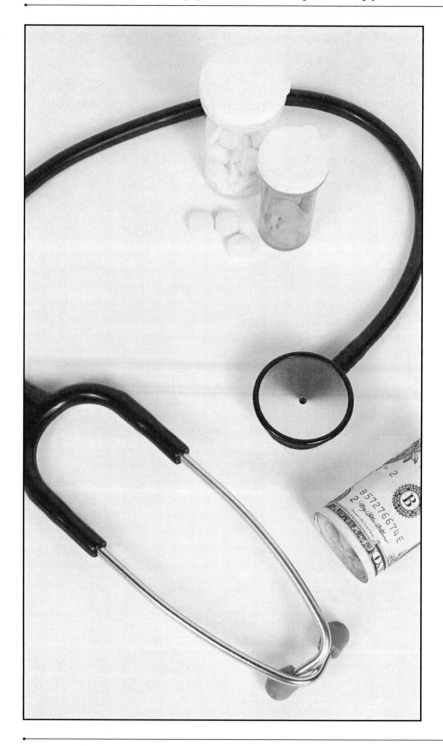

H

Hazard *(General Insurance Terms)* — A particular situation that augments the chance of a loss happening because of a peril, or adding to the severity of the loss.

Health benefits package *(Health Insurance)* — The benefits offered to the policyholders of a health plan.

Health care financing administration *(Health Insurance)* — The specific division of the department of health and human services that oversees Medicare and Medicaid. They are also responsible for creating the guidelines medical care providers must meet to be certified.

Health history *(Health Insurance)* — A tool used in the underwriting of a health care policy to determine whether they are acceptable risks.

Health insurance *(Health Insurance)* — A plan that covers or shares the expenses associated with health care. These plans fall into three classifications: commercial health insurance, which is provided by many different companies; private noncommercial health insurance, which is provided by Blue Cross and Blue Shield; and social insurance, which is provided by social security.

Health Insurance Association of America *(Health Insurance)* — A group that promotes health insurance through generating publicity, research, and education on the subject. This group is backed by insurers.

Health maintenance organization *(Health Insurance)* — A prepaid plan that provides medical services to members. Health care providers contract with this type of plan to provide services to members. The plan members must then seek services from these providers. Employers who have more than 25 employees are obligated to offer them an HMO plan, except if the cost exceeds that of the currently offered benefit plans.

Health plan *(Health Insurance)* — A term that refers to any plan that offers medical services to its members.

Health services agreement *(Health Insurance)* — The arrangement made between an employer and an insurer detailing the specifics of a plan; for example, benefits, enrollment, and eligibility.

High-pressure tactics *(Health Insurance)* — The illegal use of threats, physical intimidation, fear, or coercion to sell insurance policies. These types of tactics are often used in the marketing of policies supplementing Medicare.

Highly protected risk *(Property Insurance)* — A risk that is covered under a lower rate, due to above average construction and fire sprinklers.

Hired automobile *(Vehicle Insurance)* — A car that does not belong to the insured, members of their household, or their employees. It is leased, borrowed, or rented by the insured.

Hold harmless agreement *(Liability Insurance)* — A contract stating that one party will assume the inherent risks in a situation. This removes potential liability from the other party. This type of agreement is usually included as part of a lease or easement.

Holographic will *(Estate)* — A handwritten, signed will that is found to be valid and legal.

Home health agency *(Health Insurance)* — An agency approved by and contracted to a health plan to provide certain services.

Home health care *(Health Insurance)* — Care provided at a patient's home. This care can be provided by nurses, health care aides, or therapists, on a part-time basis.

Home health services *(Health Insurance)* — Home health care covered by Part A of Medicare. This care is provided by a licensed agent.

Home service insurance *(Life Insurance)* — A policy of smaller value, usually $10,000 to $15,000. These policies can be paid for by bank draft or check sent by mail.

Homeowners insurance *(Property Insurance)* — A policy that insures the policyholder against liability stemming from the perils they may experience as a homeowner or renter.

Homeowners policy *(Liability Insurance/Property Insurance)* — A policy that covers hazards to a homeowner or renter of a home. These policies typically cover the homeowner and the home.

Hospice *(Health Insurance)* — A health care provider covered by Medicare Part A. Hospice provides care for patients who have a terminal disease and their families, including pain and symptom relief.

Hospital affiliation *(Health Insurance)* — An agreement between a hospital and a particular health plan, wherein the hospital provides care to the plan's members.

Hospital alliances *(Health Insurance)* — Several hospitals that have allied to share services, with the aim of reducing costs. This type of alliance helps the hospitals to stay competitive.

Hospital benefits *(Health Insurance)* — Benefits that pay for hospital visits, including the room and other costs incurred during the stay.

Hospital confinement rider *(Health Insurance)* — A rider that is optional within a disability policy. The rider does away with the normal elimination period should the insured be admitted to the hospital as an inpatient.

Hospital income insurance *(Health Insurance)* — Insurance that provides an income while the insured is in the hospital. This type of policy pays out on a weekly or monthly basis. The benefit paid out can be used to pay hospital expenses or for whatever purpose the insured chooses.

Hospital indemnity *(Health Insurance)* — A type of coverage that does not take into account the actual amount of expenses incurred through a hospital stay or other care provided by a hospital. This coverage pays out on a regular basis, for example, weekly or monthly.

Hospital insurance *(Health Insurance)* — Under Part A of Medicare, coverage for inpatient hospital stays, home health care provided by a nurse, and hospice care. Some services require a co-payment or deductible.

Hospital tax *(Health Insurance)* — A tax on income mandated by social security. The money collected by this tax is used to pre-pay Medicare Part A costs.

Hospitalization expense policy *(Health Insurance)* — A policy that provides coverage for inpatient hospital stays and expenses incurred during the stay; for example, X-rays and blood work. Coverage may also be provided for emergency care and surgical costs.

Hospitalization insurance *(Health Insurance)* — Insurance that covers specific expenses incurred during a hospital stay caused by injury or illness. Only expenses falling under a certain limit, specified in the contract, are covered.

House confinement *(Health Insurance)* — A clause in some policies that states the insured must be under home confinement to be covered. This clause is usually found in loss of income policies.

Household personal property *(Property Insurance)* — Under a farm property coverage form, this term is used to distinguish the property of a farm's residents from the farm's property. Personal property may include household items, furnishings and personal items.

Housekeeping *(General Insurance Terms)* — A factor considered in underwriting certain types of policies; for example, property insurance. The term refers to the care and upkeeping of a property.

HR-10 *(Pensions)* — A retirement plan, also called the Keogh Act Plan. This plan is designed for the self-employed.

Human life value *(Life Insurance)* — A way of deciding how much life insurance an individual may need. The person's income, expenses, and years remaining in the workplace are considered, as well as the depreciating value of the dollar.

H

I

Identification card *(Health Insurance)* — A card issued to each member of a health care plan. This card is presented at the time of a medical service to identify the person as being covered by an insurer.

Identification of benefits *(Health Insurance)* — Reimbursement of the cost of finding and entrusting the care of a disabled insured to their relatives.

If clauses *(Property Insurance)* — A clause stating that coverage will be discontinued if the insured is found to be doing certain things; for example, withholding pertinent information.

Illegal occupation provision *(Health Insurance)* — A clause that states the insured is not covered for losses that arise if he or she tries to commit a felony. Coverage is also voided if the insured is working at an illegal occupation.

Immature policies *(Liability Insurance)* — A claims made on a policy that has been in effect for less than five years. When being rated, a discount on the manual rates for these policies.

Immediate vesting *(Liability Insurance/Property Insurance)* — Under immediate vesting, the insured may begin collecting benefits right away. This is typically only done in pension plans.

Impaired insurer *(General Insured Terms)* — An insurer who is experiencing financial trouble and having difficulty paying all obligations and requirements.

Impaired property *(Liability Insurance)* — A piece of property that includes the insured's defective or subpar work, and because of this, can no longer be used or is less useful. This property may also be less useful because the insured did not complete a contractual obligation.

Impaired risk *(Health Insurance/ Life Insurance)* — A risk or prospective insured in less-desirable conditions; for example, a health insurance applicant who has had several heart attacks.

Impairment of capital *(General Insurance Terms)* — A situation wherein the surplus fund of a stock insurer has been depleted to the point where the insurer has to invade the accounts made up of stockholder contributions to pay their liabilities. This is permitted in some locations and not permitted in others.

Implied authority *(General Insurance Terms)* — The authority that a member of the public may believe an agent to have. For example, if an agent is repeatedly seen signing contracts on behalf of the agency, though he or she may not have authority to do so, it is reasonable for the public to believe the agent has that authority.

Implied warranty *(Legal Terminology)* — A warranty that has not been put into writing but has been implied by one party.

Improvements and betterments *(Property Insurance)* —
Enhancements or modifications made to a building by the person
leasing it. These changes add to the value of the building.

Imputed *(Legal Terminology)* — When the acts performed by
one person are deemed to be the acts of another. Most often this
occurs when the actions of the agent are deemed to be those of
the principal.

In-area services *(Health Insurance)* — Health care services that
are offered in a geographical area designated in the contract.

In kind *(Property Insurance)* — The replacement of a damaged
item with a new or comparable item instead of a cash payout.

Incidents of ownership *(Liability Insurance)* — The rights of
the policy owner as listed in the policy; for example, the right to
choose a new beneficiary.

Income policy *(Liability Insurance)* — A policy that pays a
benefit out monthly to provide an income for the policyholder,
instead of paying out a one-time benefit.

Incompetent *(Legal Terminology)* — Someone who is not able
to handle his or her own affairs due to mental incapacity, being
younger than the age of consent, or another reason.

Incontestable clause *(Health Insurance/Life Insurance)* — A
stipulation that limits the time the insurer has to dispute the
information provided in the policy contract. This clause usually
takes effect two or three years after the policy begins. In health
insurance, this clause further states that claims cannot be denied
due to a preexisting condition, except for those expressly named

in the contract. In life insurance, this clause further states that a death benefit cannot be denied due to misrepresentation by the insured of their health condition at the time he or she took the policy out.

Increased cost of construction insurance *(Property Insurance)* — Insurance that covers the extra expense associated with reconstruction, where the damaged or destroyed building must be rebuilt using more expensive resources. This is usually due to new ordinances.

Increased hazard *(Property Insurance)* — A situation that places the insured or the insured property at a greater risk for loss. For example, if the insured begins storing explosives in his or her garage, the hazard has increased.

Increasing term insurance *(Life Insurance)* — A term policy that maintains the same premium throughout the term and has an increasing death benefit.

Incurred but not reported *(General Insurance Terms)* — A term applied to losses that have already taken place but have not yet been filed as claims.

Incurred expense *(General Insurance Terms)* — Expenses that have not yet been paid for.

Incurred loss ratio *(General Insurance Terms)* — The ratio of losses sustained as compared to money earned from premiums.

Incurred losses *(General Insurance Terms)* — Losses that have been sustained during a specific time period. These losses may or may not be paid during this time period.

Indemnify *(General Insurance Terms)* — The act of returning someone who has sustained a loss to the position they were in before the loss occurred.

Indemnitor *(General Insurance Terms)* — An individual or company who agrees to assume the obligation normally placed on a surety if the person a bond was issued on defaults. This is usually done because the applicant does not qualify as an acceptable risk by the surety's standards.

Indemnity *(General Insurance Terms)* — Issuing a payment or replacement to a person who has suffered a loss.

Indemnity bond *(General Insurance Terms)* — A bond that promises to indemnify the obligee against losses stemming from the principal's failure to perform.

Independent adjuster *(General Insurance Terms)* — An adjuster who works for various insurers to scrutinize and settle claims. These adjusters are independent contractors, who may work for other types of companies.

Independent agency system *(General Insurance Terms)* — A system for the distribution of insurance through independent contractors. The agents work on a commission basis for insurers they have contracted with to sell or provide service on insurance policies.

Independent agent *(General Insurance Terms)* — Agents who work as independent contractors within the framework of the independent agency system.

Independent contractor *(General Insurance Terms)* — A person hired to work for a contracted time. The independent contractor is not considered an employee.

Index bureau experience *(General Insurance Terms)* — A method of tracking losses stemming from claims made during a year-long time frame.

Indexing year *(Health Insurance)* — The year used when calculating social security benefits. This is usually the second year prior to turning 62, death, or disability, whichever happens first.

I

Indirect loss/damage *(Property Insurance)* — Also known as a consequential loss. A loss that occurs as a result of a hazard but not directly caused by that hazard. For example, loss of a taxi due to an accident is a direct loss. Loss of income because the taxi is no longer functional is an indirect loss.

Individual account plan *(Pensions)* — A pension plan, usually a defined contribution or profit-sharing plan, which generates a separate account for each person in the plan. The benefits generated are based on the amount within each individual account, as well as the gains and losses.

Individual contract *(Health Insurance)* — A policy that covers a particular individual and may cover other members of that person's family.

Individual contract pension trust *(Pensions)* — A plan wherein the title to insurance or annuity contracts is held by a trust for the policyholders, usually employees.

Individual life insurance *(Life Insurance)* — A kind of life insurance policy where a single contract covers a single insured.

Individual Practice Association (IPA) model HMO *(Health Insurance)* — An arrangement wherein an individual practice association provides medical services from physicians they have contracted with.

Individual Retirement Account (IRA) *(Pensions)* — A retirement plan for those under the age of 70.5 (70 plus six months), which allows them to reserve up to $2,000 a year for retirement.

Individual risk premium modification rating plan *(General Insurance Terms)* — A plan wherein the premium is modified.

Industrial life insurance *(Life Insurance)* — A classification that refers to insurance sold on debits, in the amount of less than $1,000. Premiums are then collected on a regular basis, whether weekly or monthly.

Industrial risk insurers *(General Insurance Terms)* — An association of stock property insurers and casualty insurers that was formed to write insurance for risks in large amounts.

Inflation factor *(Health Insurance)* — An amount loaded into the premium to compensate for future inflation of medical costs and loss payments.

Inflation guard coverage *(Property Insurance)* — Insurance that intermittently increases in value to keep a realistic amount of coverage, due to the rapidly inflating cost of building materials.

Inflation protection *(Health Insurance)* — A stipulation in a health insurance contract that augments the amount of the benefits in anticipation of the cost of medical services rising.

In-force business *(Health Insurance/Life Insurance)* — The cumulative total of the policies that are either totally paid up or in the process of being paid. In life insurance, this amount is measured by the cumulative value of an insurer's portfolio. In health insurance, this amount is the volume of premiums of the insurer's business portfolio.

Informal plan *(Pensions)* — A plan for retirement wherein no specific benefit amount has to be paid and no source of funding is specified. Legally, under this plan, the employer has no compulsory duties and the employee has no rights.

Inherent explosion *(Property Insurance)* — An explosion that occurs as the result of a situation that exists organically at the insured's premises. For example, an explosion at a fireworks factory is inherent.

Inherent vice *(Property Insurance)* — A deficit in the property that causes it to self-destruct.

Initial eligibility period *(Health Insurance)* — A time frame during which prospective insureds can apply for insurance without having to prove insurability.

Initial premium *(General Insurance Terms)* — The premium paid at the beginning of the policy. This amount may be adjusted at the end of the contract term.

Innkeepers legal liability *(Liability Insurance)* — Insurance for hotel or motel operators that covers them against liability for the property of guests.

In-patient *(General Insurance Terms)* — An individual who has been admitted to a hospital or health care facility as a patient in residence.

Inside limits *(Health Insurance)* — Limits that apply to hospital expense benefits. These limits vary from the maximums stated in the policy contract.

Insolvency clause *(Reinsurance)* — A stipulation that states that the reinsurer is liable for a share of a loss assumed through a treaty although the insurer is now unable to meet their financial obligations.

Insolvent insurer *(General Insurance terms)* — An insurer who does not have the funds to meet all of the financial obligations it is contracted to meet.

Inspection *(General Insurance Terms)* — The process of verifying facts about a party in an insurance contract, whether a policyholder, claimant, or new applicant. This process is usually done by a commercial agency.

Inspection bureau *(Liability Insurance/Property Insurance)* — A group that investigates possible exposures and establishes rates. These groups are created by property and liability insurers.

Inspection report *(General Insurance Terms)* — A report compiled by an inspection bureau or an insurer that summarizes the features of an insured or an applicant. This can include the financial or physical aspects.

Installment refund annuity *(Annuities)* — An annuity that pays a benefit until the equivalent of the price paid for the annuity has been paid out. These benefit payments continue regardless of whether the person covered by the annuity remains alive.

Installment refund option *(Annuities)* — An option within an annuity that converts the annuity to a installment refund annuity. After choosing this option, the annuity will continue to pay benefits, even if the person covered by the annuity is deceased, until the price paid for the annuity has been paid out.

Installment settlement *(Liability Insurance)* — A term referring to the payment of a life insurance policy's benefits in installments instead of a lump sum.

Installments certain *(Life Insurance)* — An option wherein the value of a settlement is paid in equal portions for a time frame that is specified in the settlement.

Institute of life insurance *(Life Insurance)* — A part of the American Council of Life Insurance, which originated as an agency tasked with building the reputation of life insurance.

Institutional property *(Property Insurance)* — A type of property eligible for special treatment within package policies. This can include religious or charitable organizations, hospitals, and educational institutions.

Insurability *(General Insurance Terms)* — A measure of whether a person or property is an acceptable risk. An applicant who has met the standards set by an insurance company is deemed insurable.

Insurable interest *(General Insurance Terms)* — The interest an individual or company has in an insured item that would cause him or her financial harm if a loss were to occur.

Insurable risk *(General Insurance Terms)* — A risk that conforms to the following criteria: The possible loss must be plainly explained; the loss must be accidental and significant enough to be considered a hardship to the insured; the loss must also be part of a similar group of risks, so as to make the loss foreseeable; the loss must not occur at the same time as multiple others; and finally, the insurer must be able to compute the probability of a loss and a realistic cost for the insurance.

Insurance *(General Insurance Terms)* — A method of risk reduction that shifts the risks of individuals to an insurance company. In exchange for consideration, known as a premium, the insurer assumes the losses the insured may suffer. To what extent the insurer assumes the losses is clearly defined in the policy contract.

Insurance adjuster *(General Insurance Terms)* — A person charged with investigating a claim to establish whether the company is liable and to what extent. The investigation can include interviews of the parties involved, property inspections, and reviewing hospital records or police reports.

Insurance commissioner *(General Insurance Terms)* — The individual who heads the state's agency for insurance regulation. This person may also be referred to as the Director or Superintendent, depending on the state.

Insurance department *(General Insurance Terms)* — A department charged administrating the laws that govern the insurance business. This also includes licensing, examining, and regulating insurance professionals. In the United States, this is a government bureau, or a division of another government bureau. In Canada, this is done by the federal government.

Insurance examiner *(General Insurance Terms)* — The individual who administers the examining and auditing of insurers. This person is considered a representative of the state's insurance department.

§ I §

Insurance guaranty act *(General Insurance Terms)* — An act that provides funds that are used as a guaranty for policyholders in the event his or her insurer becomes insolvent.

Insurance hall of fame *(General Insurance Terms)* — An organization that selects people to honor based on the contributions they have made to insurance.

Insurance in force *(Health Insurance/ Life Insurance)* — In life insurance, the amount of the policies that remain to be paid out. In health insurance, the yearly premium due on current policies.

Insurance Institute of America *(General Insurance Terms)* — A group charged with creating programs and examinations in insurance and related subjects, such as underwriting, adjusting, and risk management.

Insurance policy *(General Insurance Terms)* — The contract between an insurance company and the insured.

Insurance regulatory examiners society *(General Insurance Terms)* — A group created with for the purpose of promoting education and cooperation between state examiners. The group also conducts examinations of insurers. This group is comprised of state regulatory examiners.

Insurance to value *(General Insurance Terms)* — An insurance contract that estimates the worth of the items insured therein.

Insured *(General Insurance Terms)* — Also known as the policyholder or the policy owner. The insured is the person whose potential losses are covered by the insurer through the contract.

Insured contract *(Liability Insurance)* — A term used to specify the limit of contractual liability coverage. This term can refer to lease agreements, easement agreements, and any other agreement that relates to the insured's business.

Insured plan *(Pensions)* — A type of retirement plan wherein benefits are guaranteed by an insurance company. This does not necessarily mean that the plan includes life insurance.

Insurer *(General Insurance Terms)* — Also known as the carrier or company. In an insurance contract, the entity that agrees to indemnify the losses of the insured.

Insuring agreement *(General Insurance Terms)* — The section of the policy contract that specifies the hazards the insured is covered against, the people covered, and the length of the contract.

Integrated LTC rider *(Health Insurance)* — A rider added to a life insurance policy stating that LTC benefits will, if paid out, reduce the amount of the policy's benefits.

Integrated plan *(Pensions)* — A type of pension plan approved by the U.S. Treasury Department, which increases benefits by a particular formula.

Intentional injury *(Health Insurance)* — An injury that occurs as the result of a willful act meant to cause harm.

Inter vivos transfer *(Legal Terminology)* — When all or a part of a person's estate is transferred before that person's death.

Inter vivos trust *(Legal Terminology)* — A trust created and made effective during the grantor's lifetime.

Interest *(General Insurance Terms)* — The rate of return earned on the premium the company has invested over the term of the policy.

Interest adjusted cost *(Life Insurance)* — A way of calculating the true cost of life insurance that accounts for the interest the money used to pay premiums would have accrued if the money had been invested.

Interest rate risk *(General Insurance Terms)* — A risk associated with investments. By investing in bonds, the investor runs the risk that he or she will purchase at a certain interest rate and the economy will improve after the purchase, making current interest rates higher than it was at the time of purchase. The investor is then locked into a lower interest rate.

Interest sensitive provision *(Life Insurance)* — A provision that guarantees a certain amount of interest plus an additional percentage if the current interest rate is higher than a certain percentage specified in the contract. This provision is usually found in flexible premium policies.

Interline endorsement *(General Insurance Terms)* — A commercial endorsement that affects more than one aspect of a package policy.

Intermediary *(Reinsurance)* — A broker specializing in reinsurance who works as a representative of the insured to settle on a reinsurance contract. Usually, the broker works with a reinsurer who pays them commissions based on the premiums ceded.

Intermediate care *(Health Insurance)* — Nursing care supervised by a physician or registered nurse, provided at a skilled nursing facility. This type of care is considered to be a step down from skilled nursing care.

Intermediate care facility *(Health Insurance)* — A state-licensed nursing care facility that cares for patients who do not require the level of care provided at a hospital or skilled nursing facility.

Intermediate report *(Health Insurance/Workers Compensation)* — A report that gives an update on the current condition of an individual with an ongoing disability.

Interrogatories *(Legal Terminology)* — A pre-trial method of evidence gathering wherein one party submits questions to the other party.

Interstate carrier *(General Insurance Terms)* — A company that provides transportation in multiple states and across state lines.

Interstate commerce commission endorsement *(Property Insurance)* — An endorsement that guarantees losses to cargo will be insured, regardless of whether the hazard causing them is covered by the policy. This endorsement is mandatory for all policies written for interstate motor carriers who are hired to haul cargo. Losses paid out under this policy caused by a hazard not listed in the policy must be repaid by the carrier.

Intervening cause *(Legal Terminology)* — Used as a defense against charges of negligence. An intervening cause interrupts the chain of events that must be established to have a proximate cause.

Intoxicants and narcotics provision *(Health Insurance)* — A provision that states the policy is not liable for losses that occur as a result of the policyholder being intoxicated or taking a narcotic without a physician's supervision and recommendation.

Invalidity *(Health Insurance)* — A term used in health insurance that is interchangeable with illness.

Investigative consumer report *(General Insurance terms)* — A report comprised of findings about the character of an insured or prospective insured. The information in the report is gathered through interviews with family, friends, colleagues, and other acquaintances.

Investment income *(General Insurance Terms)* — The amount insurers earn from their investments. This amount can include interest payments, stock dividends, and profits made on stocks sold, known as realized capital gains.

Investment reserve *(General Insurance Terms)* — The assets an insurance company has put aside to compensate for a reduction in the value of the securities the company owns.

Involuntary unemployment insurance *(General Insurance Terms)* — A type of insurance that pays the policyholder's creditors should the policyholder be unemployed against his or her will; for example, because of layoffs, strike, or lockout.

Iron safe clause *(Property Insurance)* — A clause stating that the insured must keep records in a safe.

Irrevocable beneficiary *(Life Insurance)* — A designation of beneficiary that can only be changed with that person's consent.

Irrevocable trust *(Legal Terminology)* — A trust that cannot be revoked by the individual who established it.

Issued business *(Life Insurance)* — Contracts that have already been written but have not yet been agreed to by the insured.

Item *(General Insurance Terms)* — A general term that can be used to refer to an individual piece of property that is listed as covered within a policy. This can also mean a schedule within a policy that lists all the property that is insured.

J

Jewelers block insurance policy *(Property Insurance)* — A policy that covers the property of jewelers and the property of others in their care or custody against the most probable types of losses.

Jewelry floater *(Property Insurance)* — A policy that covers specified jewelry against all risks. The amount each piece is insured for is usually specified in the policy.

Joint and survivorship option *(Life Insurance)* — An option within a life insurance policy that allows the value of the policy to be disbursed in a joint and survivorship annuity.

Joint annuity *(Life Insurance)* — An annuity purchased in the names of two people and paid to them until one dies. At the time that one person dies, the annuity is terminated.

Joint control *(Estate)* — Control of the items that make up an estate by a bonding company, also known as a surety, and an administrative party, such as an executor, known as the fiduciary. Any funds are put in joint accounts and dispensed only with the consent of both the surety and the fiduciary.

Joint insurance *(Life Insurance)* — A policy written in the names of at least two people. Benefits are only paid on the occasion of the first death.

Joint insured *(Life Insurance)* — An individual named in a joint insurance contract.

Joint liability *(Liability Insurance)* — Liability for which more than one person is responsible.

Joint tenancy *(Legal Terminology)* — A form of property ownership wherein at least two people are equal owners. If one should die, the other assumes total ownership.

Joint underwriting association *(General Insurance Terms)* — An association comprised of insurance companies, which exists to provide a type of insurance to the general public. The individuals who insure under this kind of association pay the usual premiums as well as assessments. The money generated by the assessments funds the association's operating costs.

Joint-survivor option *(Annuities)* — An option available within an annuity contract, which offers a guaranteed income to the annuitant. Once the annuitant is deceased, his or her beneficiary is provided an income.

Jumping juvenile *(Life Insurance)* — A term used to refer to a policy written on a child, typically in units of $1,000. If the child turns 21, the value of the policy is automatically increased without any extra proof of insurability, such as a medical examination, required.

Juvenile insurance *(Life Insurance)* — An insurance policy written on a child under the age of 21.

Keogh Act plan *(Life Insurance)* — Also referred to as a HR-10 plan. A plan that allows those who are self-employed to set up a retirement plan and have access to tax benefits comparative to the benefits offered in corporate pensions. This plan was established under the Self-Employed Individual's Tax Retirement Act.

Key employee insurance *(Health Insurance/Life Insurance)* — In health insurance, a policy that offers salary continuation or medical care to a key employee. The premiums for this plan are paid in part or totally by the employer. In life insurance, a policy payable to the employer that covers the life of a key employee whose death would cause the employer a financial hardship.

Key person insurance *(Life Insurance)* — In health insurance, a policy that offers salary continuation or medical care to a key employee. The premiums for this plan are paid in part or totally by the employee. In life insurance, a policy payable to the employer that covers the life of a key employee whose death would cause the employer a financial hardship.

Kidnapping coverage *(Criminal)* — Insurance that covers the peril of an individual being captured against his or her will, outside of the insured's premises, and forced to collude in a criminal act, either by opening a safe or giving the robber the pertinent information to do so. This type of coverage is often included in a package crime policy.

Kidnap-ransom insurance *(Criminal)* — A form of coverage that exists in only a few markets, without standard rates. This type of coverage protects a financial institution in the event that it has to pay ransom for an employee who is named in the contract.

K

L

Landlords protective liability *(Liability Insurance)* — Insurance that covers a property owner acting as a landlord by renting his property to a tenant.

Lapse *(General Insurance Terms)* — The cancellation of a policy due to the non-payment of the premium due.

Lapse ratio *(Life Insurance)* — In life insurance, a ratio that measures the amount of contracts lapsed in a certain time period. The ratio measures the contracts that have lapsed to the total number that were in effect.

Lapsed policy *(General Insurance Terms)* — A policy that has been cancelled due to lack of payment of the premiums.

Large claim pooling *(Health Insurance)* — A system wherein claims over a specified amount are placed in a pool. The pool is made up of claims charged by several smaller groups. This is done to help curb fluctuations in premium amounts in these smaller groups.

Laser beam endorsement *(Liability Insurance)* — An endorsement that allows insurers to exclude particular exposures.

Last clear chance *(Legal Terminology)* — A principle wherein an individual who had a final clear opportunity to circumvent an accident and does not do so can be liable for the accident.

Latent defect *(General Insurance Terms)* — A defect that does not present itself right away.

Law of large numbers *(General Insurance Terms)* — A law about the probability of loss, which states that a larger number of exposures will come closer to the probable amount of loss.

Leader location *(Property Insurance)* — Under business income insurance, one of the four kinds of dependent properties covered. A site that attracts customers to the insured's business.

Leasehold interest coverage form *(Property Insurance)* — A form of commercial property coverage. If a lease is broken due to property damage stemming from a peril specified in the contract, the difference between the amount of rent paid and the total rental value is paid for the term of the lease.

Leasehold interest insurance *(Property Insurance)* — Property insurance form that covers the loss of lease income due to damage to the property caused by an insured peril.

Ledger cost *(Life Insurance)* — The net cost of a life insurance policy. This amount is determined by deducting the value of the policy at the end of the year from the total amount of premiums paid, minus dividends.

Legal expense insurance *(Liability Insurance)* — Insurance that provides policyholders with legal services. These services are paid for according to a schedule.

Legal hazard *(Legal Terminology)* — A rise in the chance of a loss due to legal action.

Legal liability *(Legal Terminology)* — Legal liability that does not stem from a contract or legal agreement. For insurance purposes, this type of liability arises from a person injuring another person negligently.

Legal reserve *(Liability Insurance)* — The minimum amount needed for a life insurance policy, as dictated by the laws of a specific area.

Legal reserve life insurance company *(Life Insurance)* — A life insurance company that sustains the reserve amount mandated by the laws of the area in which it operates.

Legend drug *(Health Insurance)* — A drug bearing a label that says "Caution: Federal law prohibits dispensing without a prescription."

Legislated coverages *(General Insurance Terms)* — Coverages that are offered by institutions that exist due to federal or state laws, such as Flood Insurance or Medicare.

Legislative risk *(General Insurance Terms)* — A risk wherein modifications to taxation laws may cause negative effects on an individual's investments.

Length of stay *(Health Insurance)* — The total length, in days, that an insured stays in a hospital or similar medical facility.

Lessee's safe deposit box coverage form *(Criminal)* — Insurance that covers the loss of items kept inside the insured's safe deposit box in a depository facility, such as a bank. This commercial crime form does not cover money kept in a safe deposit box.

Level commission system *(General Insurance Terms)* — Commission system wherein premiums on new contracts and renewed contracts receive the same percentage of the premiums.

Level death benefit option *(Life Insurance)* — An option in universal life insurance that furnishes either the face value of the policy upon the insured's death or a specified percentage of the accumulation value.

Level premium insurance *(Life Insurance)* — A form of insurance under which the premium does not change throughout the term of the policy. Generally, the majority of life insurance policies are paid in this manner.

L

Level term insurance *(Life Insurance)* — A term life policy whose death benefit and premiums remain the same for the term of the contract.

Liabilities *(General Insurance Terms)* — A term for money that is currently owed or that will be owed in the future.

Liability insurance *(Liability Insurance)* — Insurance that covers the insured against a loss that stems from his responsibility to other people. This responsibility can be compulsory under the law or implied in a contract.

Liability limits *(Liability Insurance)* — The maximum benefit available for payout in a liability insurance policy.

Libel *(Legal Terminology)* — A statement made in print about an individual that is untrue and hurtful. The exception to this is under maritime law, wherein this term means a legal action taken against the owner of a ship.

Libel insurance *(Liability Insurance)* — Insurance that covers the insured against legal action taken due to a statement he has written that is thought to be libelous.

Liberalization clause *(Property Insurance)* — A clause stipulating that the policy will be changed to accommodate the changes mandated by legislation or rating authorities. In order for this clause to apply, no extra premium must be required.

License *(General Insurance Terms)* — A document, most often issued by the state, that proves the bearer's authority to work as an agent or insurer.

License and permit bonds *(Surety)* — A bond mandated by the state or other ruling jurisdiction to be acquired by people working in certain occupations; for example, plumbers. The bond guarantees the bearer will comply with the governing laws. Should the bearer fail to comply, the bond identifies him or her.

Licensee *(Legal Terminology)* — A person who is authorized to enter the property of another for his or her own gain. The property owner must advise this person of any hidden hazards on the property and otherwise exercise care not to injure him or her.

Lien *(Legal Terminology)* — A claim against property, brought by a worker or creditor who has not received the appropriate payment.

Lien plan *(Liability Insurance)* — A rarely issued type of coverage under which a substandard risk is insured, but less than the full policy benefit is paid out if the insured dies before a certain time.

Life annuity *(Annuities)* — An annuity that supplies the insured with a lifelong income, which is paid on a regular basis.

Life conservation *(Liability Insurance)* — The administration of attempts to conserve human lives by means of research, lawmaking, and increasing public awareness.

Life expectancy *(Liability Insurance)* — The average amount of years remaining in a person's life, using the mortality table as a reference.

Life expectancy term insurance *(Liability Insurance)* — Term life insurance that is issued for the amount of years the insured expects to live. This differs from an ordinary life insurance policy, which is typically issued to a specific age, often 65 years.

Life income *(Liability Insurance)* — An option available under a settlement agreement wherein the beneficiary is paid in installments for the rest of his or her life, even if the principal amount is already exhausted.

Life insurance *(Life Insurance)* — A system of sharing risk that pays a specified amount of benefits if the insured dies. Depending on the terms specified in the plan, the insured may receive benefits under other circumstances, such as disability.

Life insurance cost surrender index *(Life Insurance)* — An index that establishes the guaranteed cash surrender value of a life insurance policy, which is shown to potential insureds. The index gives the value of the policy if surrendered at the 10- or 20-year mark, with interest on any applicable dividends calculated at 5 percent.

Life insurance trust *(Life Insurance)* — A life insurance policy that names a trust company as a the beneficiary. Benefits are issued under the agreement made with the trust company.

Life insurers' conference *(Life Insurance)* — An organization comprised of life insurers. This organization allows for the exchange of information on management and management issues between these insurers.

Life paid up at age *(Life Insurance)* — Life insurance that covers the insured for his or her lifetime, but stops payment of premiums at a given age to pay up the policy.

Life underwriter *(Life Insurance)* — A risk appraiser or life insurance agent.

Limit of liability *(Liability Insurance)* — The maximum benefit for which the insurer is liable, as established in the contract.

Limit of liability rule *(Property Insurance)* — A method of apportioning a loss among several insurers that all cover the same property.

Limitations *(General Insurance Terms)* — Limits and exceptions to the coverage provided in the contract, for example, the limit of liability stated in the contract.

Limited agent *(General Insurance Terms)* — An agent who can only deal in a certain form of insurance, for example, travel insurance. In certain states, this type of agent does not have to meet education and licensing requirements.

Limited health insurance *(Health Insurance)* — Health insurance that only covers certain illnesses or injuries as specified in the contract.

Limited partnership *(General Insurance Terms)* — A partnership of at least two people who manage a business together to earn a profit. One or more of the partners is considered the limited partner because he or she does not operate the business on a daily basis, but still has an investment in the business and a vote in the way it is managed. This partner has limited liability.

Limited payment life *(Life Insurance)* — Insurance that covers the insured's whole life. Premiums are only paid for the amount of years specified.

Limited payment whole life *(Life Insurance)* — A policy that permits the insured to pay the entire premium quicker than the traditional model.

Limited policies *(Health Insurance/Life Insurance)* — Policies that only pay in the event of certain occurrences as specified in the contract. In health insurance, this term can be used to refer to a contract with low limits and limited forms.

Limited pollution liability coverage form *(Liability Insurance)* — A commercial form that offers pollution liability coverage if a claim is made, but does not offer coverage of clean-up expenses.

Limited theft coverage endorsement *(Property Insurance)* — A form that protects occupants of a home who are not the owners against theft.

Limits *(General Insurance Terms)* — The maximum benefit that will be paid out as a result of a loss. This term can also refer to the age at which an insurer will not issue a policy or will no longer continue a policy.

Line *(General Insurance Terms)* — A general term that can be used in various ways. This term can be used to refer to a specific kind of insurance; for example, the property insurance line. This term can also be used to group all the policies written for the same insured. Lastly, this can also mean the amount of coverage written for a certain property; for example, a $50,000 line of property insurance.

Line card *(Property Insurance)* — A record of property insurance sold to an insured.

Line of business *(General Insurance Terms)* — A general category applied to insurers; for example, Homeowners, Health or Life.

Line sheet *(General Insurance Terms)* — A schedule used as a guide that helps ceding companies to determine the limit of liability they will undertake on different kinds of risks. This schedule lists the liability limits to be written by insurers for different risks.

Line slip *(Health Insurance)* — A document written by a broker that describes a prospective risk. The document is given to underwriters, who then decide what fraction of the risk they are willing to insure.

Lines *(Reinsurance)* — The amount a reinsurer agrees to accept in a surplus treaty.

Liquidation of insurer *(General Insurance Terms)* — Dissolution of an insurer who can no longer meet financial obligations and will not be able to meet them in the future.

Liquidity *(General Insurance Terms)* — The conversion of the insurer's non-monetary assets into cash with which claims can be paid.

Livery use *(Vehicle Insurance)* — Using a rented vehicle to carry passengers. This is usually excluded from automobile insurance policies.

Livestock coverage form *(Property Insurance)* — A commercial form used to insure livestock. This form is usually attached to farm coverage.

Livestock insurance *(Property Insurance)* — Insurance that provides a lump sum benefit to the insured if an animal listed in the policy dies from one of the perils specified in the contract.

Livestock mortality insurance *(Property Insurance)* — Insurance on livestock that is essentially life insurance for animals.

Livestock transit insurance *(Property Insurance)* — Insurance that covers accidents that kill or cripple livestock as they are being transported by rail, truck, or other comparable means.

Living benefits rider *(Health Insurance)* — A rider that provides long-term care benefits for an insured person who is terminally ill, when attached to a life insurance contract.

Living need benefits *(Health Insurance)* — A mixture of life insurance and long-term care coverage that permits life insurance to produce long-term care benefits. This practice reduces the value of the life insurance policy, because the funds used for medical expenses are deducted from the life insurance policy's death benefit.

Living trust *(Estate)* — Sometimes called an inter vivos trust. A trust created by a living person.

Lloyd's of London *(General Insurance Terms)* — Lloyd's of London is a facility under which separate insurers can accept or reject to insure the risks presented to them by a broker. Many important precedents for the insurance industry are set by Lloyd's.

Lloyd's Association *(General Insurance Terms)* — A group organized in the same manner as Lloyd's of London, which is unaffiliated with the English institution. Individuals who are not in business together come together and each is only responsible for the portion of the risk they choose to insure.

Lloyd's broker *(General Insurance Terms)* — A person who is authorized to offer prospective risks to and negotiate with the underwriters at Lloyd's.

Lloyd's syndicate *(General Insurance Terms)* — A group of Lloyd's underwriters, with one person accepting or rejecting risks on the group's behalf.

Loading *(General Insurance Terms)* — An amount that is built in to the insurance cost. This amount covers the operating cost of the insurer, as well as the chance that the insurer's losses for that period will be higher than anticipated, and the changes in the interest earned from the insurer's investments. This is added to the amount required to cover losses, known as the pure insurance cost.

Loan value *(Life Insurance)* — The amount the insured can borrow against the cash value of his or her life insurance policy.

Local agent *(General Insurance Terms)* — An agent who works on behalf of the insurance companies in a small territory in a sales and service capacity. The agent is an independent contractor who earns commission on sales.

Long term care (LTC) *(Health Insurance)* — A term that can refer to health or social care administered by health care professionals to people with diseases or disabilities.

Long term care facility *(Health Insurance)* — A facility where nursing or custodial care is provided on a long-term basis. This type of facility is usually licensed by the state.

Long term care insurance *(Health Insurance)* — Health insurance that pays out a daily benefit upon the insured becoming a resident in a nursing home.

Long term disability *(Health Insurance)* — A disability condition that persists over a long period of time.

Long term disability insurance *(Health Insurance)* — A policy that covers a longer period, usually until the insured turns 65.

Loss *(General Insurance Terms)* — A general term used to refer to the amount of a claim filed by the insured. This term can also mean the amount the insured's property value decreased as a result of a loss. This term can also refer to the amount an insurer has paid on behalf of an insured.

Loss adjustment expense *(General Insurance Terms)* — The total expenses associated with adjusting a claim. The actual amount of the loss is not included in this amount.

Loss assessment charge *(Liability Insurance/ Property Insurance)* — The insured's portion of the total amount owed to a homeowners association or other group made up of property owners due to property damage. Certain homeowners insurance policies may offer coverage for this type of charge.

Loss constant *(General Insurance Terms)* — An amount intended to offset the larger-than-average losses most smaller risks have as compared to other risks in the same classification.

Loss control *(General Insurance Terms)* — Actions performed by the insured to reduce the chance of a loss or the extent of a loss, for example, locking valuables in a safe or keeping fire extinguishers in a home or business.

Loss development *(General Insurance Terms)* — The difference between the value of the losses estimated by the insurer and the amount reported on a later date.

Loss development factor *(Workers Compensation)* — A factor introduced to give the insurer extra money to permit development of losses and reimburse them for claims reported late.

Loss expectancy *(General Insurance Terms)* — An estimate of the most likely maximum loss that could be paid out on an exposure. Special attention is given to the loss prevention measures the insured takes.

Loss frequency *(General Insurance Terms)* — The total amount of times that a loss occurs in a particular time frame.

Loss limitation *(Workers Compensation)* — Used in retrospective rating formulas. Designed to limit the amount of catastrophic losses that would usually be reported in full while calculating the final premium.

Loss loading *(Reinsurance)* — A factor used on a pure loss cost to produce a reinsurance rate.

Loss of income benefits *(Health Insurance)* — Benefits for those who are unable to work due to a disability. The loss of income may be current or in the future.

Loss of income insurance *(Health Insurance)* — Insurance that covers the insured in the case of lost income.

Loss of market *(Property Insurance)* — The loss of the opportunity to sell a specific item to a potential buyer. Certain contracts have a specific exclusion that pertains to this circumstance, however, most consider it excluded as a standard business peril.

Loss of use insurance *(Property Insurance)* — Insurance that covers the loss of use of a property due to an insured peril.

Loss payable clause *(Property Insurance)* — A clause authorizing payment to people with an insurable interest in the property, even if they are not named as the insured. This clause protects the lender in the case of a mortgage.

Loss payee *(General Insurance Terms)* — The person benefits should be paid to if a loss occurs, for example, the mortgagee of a home or property.

Loss prevention engineer *(Liability Insurance)* — The person on the insurer's staff charged with loss prevention through reduction of possible future claims.

Loss prevention service *(Liability Insurance/Property Insurance)* — The elimination or reduction of hazardous conditions with the goal of preventing losses. This is done through inspections and engineering efforts by the insurer or an outside organization.

Loss ratio *(General Insurance Terms)* — A ratio determined by dividing the losses by the premiums paid. The losses can be either losses incurred or losses paid, and the premiums can be earned premiums or written premiums.

Loss reserve *(General Insurance Terms)* — The insurer's estimated total liability for claims that have not yet been paid or losses that have occurred during a certain time frame. This amount usually also includes losses incurred but not yet reported, losses that are due but that have not been paid yet, and amounts that are not yet due.

Loss severity *(General Insurance Terms)* — The amount of a loss in financial terms.

Losses incurred *(General Insurance Terms)* — A measure of the insurer's losses in a specific time frame. This includes paid and unpaid losses.

Losses outstanding *(General Insurance Terms)* — The claims not yet settled by an insurer, expressed in a summary statement.

Losses paid *(General Insurance Terms)* — The claims that have been paid.

Lost policy release *(General Insurance Terms)* — A statement that is typically signed after the insurer has initiated a replacement policy. This statement releases the insurer from a lost or misplaced contract.

Lost wages *(General Insurance Terms)* — Potential earnings the insured was unable to receive due to an injury or disability.

Lump sum *(Life Insurance)* — A settlement option wherein the insured or beneficiary chooses to accept the entire payout amount at once instead of in regular installments.

M

Maintenance bond *(Surety)* — A type of construction bond that guarantees against defective materials or craftsmanship. This bond is good for a specified amount of time after the finished work has been accepted.

Major hospitalization policy *(Health Insurance)* — A policy that is essentially the same as major medical insurance, but that only covers expenses from the time the insured is hospitalized.

Major medical insurance *(Health Insurance)* — A kind of health insurance policy that carries a high deductible and covers most medical expenses. This type of policy limits the amount that will be paid for specific expenses, such as a hospital room, and a clause that requires a certain percentage participation.

Malicious mischief *(General Insurance Terms)* — An act comparable to vandalism, defined as intentionally damaging property that belongs to another person.

Malinger *(General Insurance Terms)* — To misrepresent the extent and severity of a disability in order to continue to collect benefits longer than needed.

Malpractice *(Liability Insurance)* — Improper conduct on the part of a professional or a deficiency of skills that can cause the professional to be legally liable.

Malpractice insurance *(Liability Insurance)* — Insurance that covers a medical practitioner in the event he or she is charged with malpractice. The insurance will pay damages as ordered by the court, and defend the insured in suits brought against them.

Managed care *(Health Insurance)* — A plan that aims to manage the employer's health care expenses by establishing guidelines for care providers and better methods for the employees to choose a provider.

Managed health care plan *(Health Insurance)* — A plan that usually includes multiple providers who split the financial risks of the plan. The plan itself finances and provides medical care services.

Management expense *(Reinsurance)* — According to a contingent commission agreement, an amount taken to cover reinsurers' overhead costs.

Manager *(General Insurance Terms)* — A title generally given to the person heading an insurance agency's branch office. The manager is usually a salaried employee who also receives a bonus based on the volume of business conducted with the agency.

Mandated benefits *(Health Insurance)* — Benefits that are legally required, whether by state or federal law.

Mandated providers *(Health Insurance)* — By law, health care providers whose services must be included.

Mandatory retirement *(Pensions)* — A retirement age mandated by a pension plan. When the insured reaches this age, he or she must retire, regardless of willingness to do so.

Manual *(General Insurance Terms)* — A guide to rates and classifications under a certain type of insurance.

Manual excess *(Liability Insurance)* — The premium for an insurance amount in excess of the liability limit. This premium is established by multiplying the manual rate by rate factors, found on a table, to determine a premium for the limit selected.

Manual rates *(General Insurance Terms)* — Insurance rates derived from data on average claims from a large amount of claims. These rates are then customized based on the information available on certain groups.

Manufacturers and contractors liability insurance *(Liability Insurance)* — A form that covers contractors or manufacturers, wherein premiums are based on payroll amounts.

Manufacturers output policy *(Property Insurance)* — Insurance that covers a manufacturer's personal property. The property is usually covered against all perils but only away from the manufacturer's premises, because this type of coverage was initially meant for products that were sent to other companies for processing.

Manufacturer's selling price clause *(Property Insurance)* — A clause under which finished goods that have yet to be sold are valued at the selling price at the time a loss occurs.

Manufacturing location *(Property Insurance)* — A location contracted to produce product, which is then delivered to the insured's consumers. Under business income coverage, one of the four categories of dependent properties.

Manuscript policy *(General Insurance Terms)* — A policy specifically written to include coverage or conditions not included in a standard policy. This type of policy is usually prepared by a larger brokerage for a larger account, in compliance with state laws.

Map *(Property Insurance)* — For insurance purposes, a map is used to locate the geographical location of a risk and assess its character. They are also used to track how many policies have been written in a certain area, thereby avoiding a catastrophic loss.

Map clerk *(Property Insurance)* — A junior underwriter charged with tracking the insurer's exposure in a given area. This is done by entering data, such as property covered and the policy number, on maps.

Marital deduction *(Estate)* — Rule that states an unrestricted amount of qualifying property can be willed from the deceased to his or her spouse.

Marital deduction trust *(Estate)* — Under this type of trust, federal taxes on the estate are minimized and the surviving spouse is given full access to the family's assets.

Market assistance plan *(Health Insurance)* — A plan promoted by the Department of Insurance that assists buyers in purchasing specific types of difficult-to-find insurance.

Market conduct *(General Insurance Terms)* — A measure of how insurers and their agents are complying with the laws that govern the insurance business, specifically the sales and marketing, and issuance of products.

Market conduct examination *(General Insurance Terms)* — An examination conducted by the state's insurance department to evaluate the practices and operations of an insurer. This examination aims to establish the insurer's authority to conduct business in that state.

Market risk *(General Insurance Terms)* — The risk of possible loss of the money one has invested. This risk exists with any investment, because no investment is guaranteed.

Market value *(General Insurance Terms)* — The price for which a product would sell on the current market.

Market value clause *(Property Insurance)* — A clause that obligates the insurer to pay the proven market price of destroyed property, rather than its cost to the insured. This type of policy is usually written for manufacturers who have finished products.

Masonry noncombustible construction *(Property Insurance)* — Construction using masonry materials, such as brick or concrete, on the outside walls of the structure, and noncombustible materials for the roof and floor.

Mass merchandising *(General Insurance Terms)* — A practice wherein a large group of individuals, such as a group of employees, all insure with the same company, and remit premiums in a lump sum.

Master contract *(Pensions)* — The contract provided to an employer whose employees have a group contract.

Master policy *(General Insurance Terms)* — Under a group insurance policy issued for employees, the contract issued to the employer. This term can also refer to a property insurance contract issued to an insured who is able to issue certificates of coverage to others.

Master servant rule *(Legal Terminology)* — A rule that states employers must protect the public from their employees' actions. Legally, employers are held responsible for the torts committed by their employees.

Material fact *(Legal Terminology)* — For insurance purposes, this is a fact deemed so important that It would change the decision made by an insurer if it were kept hidden. Misrepresentation of a material fact can void a policy.

Mature *(Life Insurance)* — A policy is said to mature when its face value is paid out; for example, when the insured dies.

Mature policies *(Liability Insurance)* — A claims made policy that has not lapsed in the last five years. These policies can no longer receive the rating credits that are issued to immature policies.

Maturity date *(Life Insurance)* — The date upon which the face value of a life insurance policy is payable, whether due to the insured's death or an endowment.

Maturity value *(Life Insurance)* — The total amount paid to an insured at the end of an endowment or to the owner of a life insurance policy after they have lived past a specified age.

Maxi tail *(Liability Insurance)* — An extended period for reporting claims after the expiration of a claims-made liability policy.

Maximum allowable cost list *(Health Insurance)* — A list of prescriptions whose reimbursement value is based on the cost of a generic.

Maximum disability policy *(Health Insurance)* — Disability insurance that allows multiple claims for multiple different disabilities, with stated limits for each claim.

Maximum retrospective premium *(Liability Insurance/ Workers Compensation)* —Under a retrospective rating plan, the maximum amount the insured will be required to pay.

Mediation *(Legal Terminology)* — An attempt to settle a dispute, involving an impartial third party who meets with the people involved in the dispute and tries to arrive at a mutually agreeable solution.

M

Medicaid *(Health Insurance)* — A health care program administered by the individual states with funding from the federal government. Those who meet certain guidelines, including income requirements, are eligible to have medical expenses paid.

Medical examination *(Health Insurance/Life Insurance)* — A physical evaluation of a prospective insured, conducted by a doctor acting as the insured's agent.

Medical examiner *(Health Insurance/Life Insurance)* — The doctor who acts as an agent of the insurer by conducting the examination of a prospective insured.

Medical expense insurance *(Health Insurance)* — Health insurance that covers medical and surgical expenses, as well as hospital expenses.

Medical expense reimbursement plan *(Health Insurance)* — A plan that issues reimbursement of specified health care-related expenses for employees.

Medical information bureau *(Health Insurance/Life Insurance)* — A bureau that keeps coded information on the health conditions of individuals who have been insured in the past. Life and health insurers subscribe to these bureaus to get all possible information on prospective insureds.

Medical loss ratio *(Health Insurance)* — A ratio calculated as total benefits divided by total premium.

Medical payments insurance *(Vehicle Insurance/Liability Insurance)* — An optional coverage under most automobile insurance policies and some other forms of liability insurance. This coverage pays for health care costs regardless of who has been assigned fault.

Medical savings account *(Health Insurance)* — An account made up of employer contributions, derived from a portion of the employee's premium payments. This account can be used by the employee to pay for any medical expenses, with the remainder eligible for cash withdrawal.

Medical supplies *(Health Insurance)* — Items deemed necessary for the treatment of an illness or injury.

Medically necessary *(Health Insurance)* — A procedure or treatment that is found to be necessary for a patient's treatment and could worsen the patient's situation if not carried out.

Medicare *(Health Insurance)* — A government run and funded plan for paying hospital and other health care costs for those who qualify. These people are usually older than 65. Coverage is divided into Part A, which provides the compulsory hospital benefits, and Part B, a voluntary program that covers medical expenses.

Medicare beneficiary *(Health Insurance)* — Anyone determined by the Social Security Administration to be eligible for Medicare benefits.

Medicare select policy *(Health Insurance)* — A supplement policy or certificate issued by Medicare that only pays benefits to certain providers that are in the network.

M

Medicare supplement insurance *(Health Insurance)* — Insurance that supplements the coverage provided by Medicare. These supplements sometimes pay the insured's deductibles or co-payments, but cannot duplicate the benefits provided to the insured by Medicare.

Member *(Health Insurance/Pensions)* — In health insurance, any person who is covered by a health plan is referred to as a member, whether he or she is the person enrolled or that person's dependent. In pensions, this term refers to an employee who is qualified to be covered under a pension plan.

Member certificate *(Health Insurance)* — A synonym for a certificate of coverage.

Member month *(Health Insurance)* — The amount of participants who are considered members each month.

Mental health provider *(Health Insurance)* — Care providers including social workers, psychologists, and psychiatrists. These people meet the federal and/or state requirements to provide mental health care.

Mental health services/supplies *(Health Insurance)* — Supplies needed to treat mental illness, substance abuse, or alcoholism.

Mental/emotional distress *(General Insurance Terms)* — A psychological condition that is usually covered if it occurs as the result of an accident.

Mercantile risk *(Property Insurance)* — A term that refers to a retail or wholesale risk as opposed to a manufacturing or service risk.

Merit rating *(General Insurance Terms)* — A rating plan most often used in personal automobile insurance. Under this plan, the insured's premium amount is dictated by the insured's loss record.

Messenger *(Criminal)* — A term usually used in commercial crime insurance. The person who has possession of the insured's property in any location other than the insured's land. This may be the insured, their employees, or their partner.

Messenger robbery insurance *(Criminal)* — Insurance that covers money and other property that is in the care of a person leaving the premises; for example, an employee delivering items to a customer.

Midi tail *(Liability Insurance)* — An extended reporting period that allows for the making of claims after a claims made liability policy has expired. This five-year extension only applies to claims that arise from events reported no more than 60 days after the policy's end.

Mill construction *(Property Insurance)* — Construction that meets particular specifications or standards that are higher than average. Buildings such as warehouses that meet these standards qualify for reduced rates on fire insurance

Million Dollar Round Table *(Life Insurance)* — An association for life insurance agents who have qualified for membership by selling a minimum of $1 million of coverage. Other criteria include that the agent be a member of the National Association of Life Underwriters.

Mini tail *(Liability Insurance)* — A 60-day extension to the reporting time frame of a policy. This automatic extension allows the insured to make claims after a claims made policy has expired.

Minimum amount policy *(Life Policy)* — A policy that only specifies a minimum face value.

Minimum compensation level *(Pensions)* — The amount of pay an employee must earn to qualify to take part in a pension plan or profit sharing plan.

Minimum deposit policy *(Life Insurance)* — A policy that carries a first-year loan value, which the insured is able to borrow

M

against as soon as the first-year premiums are paid. This is not usually done with life insurance policies.

Minimum premium *(Health Insurance/General Insurance Terms)* — In health insurance, this term refers to an arrangement wherein the fraction of the premium that the employer pays is used to cover administration costs. The rest is saved by the insurer and eventually used to pay claims. This can also refer to a general insurance term used to mean the lowest premium an insured can be covered for under a certain policy.

Minimum rate *(Property Insurance)* — A rate assigned to low-peril risks.

Minimum retrospective premium *(Liability Insurance/Workers Compensation)* — A premium used in a retrospective rating plan. This premium is the smallest amount the insured can pay under a given plan, no matter the amount of the losses incurred.

Miscellaneous benefits *(Health Insurance)* — Benefits that cover most medical costs incurred while the insured receives treatment as an inpatient. These benefits, usually provided by a group health policy, will not cover surgical costs or room and board.

Miscellaneous expenses *(Health Insurance)* — In a basic hospitalization policy, these are additional charges usually incurred during a hospital stay; for example, fees for diagnostic tests performed in the hospital. Reimbursement of this type of expense is usually limited.

Misrepresentation *(Legal Terminology)* — On the part of the insured, this term refers to providing materials to obtain a policy that do not reflect the truth. This term also refers to the insurer incorrectly explaining the terms of and benefits provided by a policy.

Misstatement of age *(Health Insurance/Life Insurance)* — The insured's supplying a false age when applying for a policy, or giving the wrong age for a beneficiary in order to receive benefits faster. This term can also refer to a clause found in life and health contracts, which details the consequences of the insurer finding out the insured misrepresented his or her age after the policy has been issued.

Mixed insurer/company *(General Insurance Terms)* — An insurer owned by both stockholders and policyholders, or an insurer who writes both life and health contracts.

Mobile agricultural machinery and equipment coverage form *(Property Insurance)* — Coverage under a commercial property form for farm machinery and equipment.

M

Mobile equipment *(Liability Insurance)* — A term refering to land vehicles that meet certain criteria: They must not be registered as a motor vehicle, they must be intended for use primarily in locations other than the public road, they must be land vehicles, and they must be mostly used on the insured's property.

Mobile home policy *(Property Insurance)* — A type of homeowners insurance that is written for a mobile home in a permanently fixed location.

Mode of premium payment *(General Insurance Terms)* — The frequency of payment the policyholder has chosen; for example, annually, monthly, or quarterly.

Modified *(General Insurance Terms)* — A general term that can be used in many contexts. Generally speaking, this term refers to a premium that has been changed from the normal premium on similar policies.

Modified adjusted gross income *(Pensions)* — An employee's adjusted gross income for a tax year, plus any tax exempt interest they have earned.

Modified community rating *(Health Insurance)* — A way of establishing the rates for specific medical expenses using data from a particular area.

Modified endowment contract *(Life Insurance)* — An endowment contract wherein the amount to be paid out after the endowment period is greater than the face value of the policy. The amount payable in the case of death is either the face value or the cash value, whichever is greater. This type of contract is taxable and subject to any penalties after tax.

Modified fee for service *(Health Insurance)* — A process wherein reimbursements for the actual cost of each procedure are made, up to a certain maximum.

Modified fire resistive construction *(Property Insurance)* — A building constructed of masonry materials or otherwise fire-resistant supplies on the outside walls, roof, and floor surfaces.

Modified life policy *(Life Insurance)* — A life insurance policy wherein the premiums are lower than normal to start and stay that way for a period of three to five years. After this time, premiums become higher than normal.

Money and securities broad form *(Criminal)* — Crime insurance form; now made obsolete by commercial crime coverage. This form covers against loss of money or securities due to various perils.

Money purchase benefit formula *(Pensions)* — A pension plan with fixed contributions for both employee and employer. Contributions are fixed based on the employee's salary, either as a flat amount or as a percentage of the salary.

Money purchase plan *(Pensions)* — A retirement or pension plan wherein a particular amount of money is used to purchase an annuity for each participating employee. This is done periodically throughout the employment, and the total of the annuities is paid out to the employee at retirement.

Monoline policy *(General Insurance Terms)* — Any single line policy coverage.

Monopolistic state fund *(Workers Compensation)* — In certain states, the law requires companies to purchase workers compensation insurance from the government. This term refers to the state-run company that exists in those states for the purpose of selling the insurance. Private insurers are prohibited from selling insurance in these states.

Monthly administration fee *(Life Insurance)* — A monthly fee assessed in universal life policies that covers the company's administrative costs.

Monthly debit ordinary (MDO) *(Life Insurance)* — Polices wherein the premiums are collected in a similar fashion to industrial policies, at the door each month.

Monthly debit ordinary status card *(Life Insurance)* — A card that indicates the monthly debit ordinary business that is still in force and has lapsed.

Moral hazard *(General Insurance Terms)* — A hazard that is caused by the morals or attitude of an insured. For example, an insured who is not morally opposed to feigning an illness to file fraudulent medical expense claims.

Morale hazard *(General Insurance Terms)* — A hazard that is based in the insured's attitude toward the insured belongings. This hazard exists when the insured no longer cares about his or her possessions because they are insured; for example, when an insured hopes to be in a car accident in order to have the insurance pay for a new car.

Morbidity *(Health Insurance)* — The comparative frequency of disease.

Morbidity rate *(Health Insurance)* — A ratio determined by comparing the frequency of illness to the amount of healthy people in a group over a certain time frame. This rate may also be calculated using the incidence of new cases or the amount of cases of a certain illness.

Morbidity table *(Health Insurance)* — A table, similar to a mortality table, that shows the frequency of illness at certain ages.

Mortality charge *(Life Insurance)* — The charge for pure insurance protection in a policy.

Mortality cost *(Life Insurance)* — In life insurance, a cost determined using the information on a mortality table. To calculate the mortality cost, the face amount of a policy is multiplied by the chance that the policy will have to be paid out as a claim, specifically, that the insured will die.

Mortality guarantee *(Annuities)* — A clause providing that the annuitant will receive an income for life, no matter the changes to the mortality rate.

Mortality rate *(Life Insurance)* — Also called the death rate. The amount of deaths in a particular group of people, which can be modified to reflect ages or causes of death. When calculated for the entire population, this rate is called the crude mortality rate.

Mortality savings *(Life Insurance)* — A number determined by deducting the actual mortality experienced from the expected mortality.

Mortality table *(Life Insurance)* — A table that displays the frequency of death at particular ages. Usually, the table also shows deaths by age group, deaths by thousands, and deaths based on a population of a million.

Mortgage *(Legal Terminology)* — An interest in a property given by the property owner, known as the mortgagee, to a lender, known as the mortgagor, in exchange for a loan of money.

Mortgage clause *(Property Insurance)* — A clause found in a direct damage policy taken on a mortgaged property. This clause specifies that reimbursement for any loss will be paid to the mortgagee, and that the mortgagee's right to recovery will not be overcome by the insured's negligence.

Mortgage holders errors and omissions coverage form *(Property Insurance)* —Commercial property form that protects mortgage holders from any losses stemming from errors or omissions.

Mortgage insurance *(Health Insurance/Life Insurance)* — A policy that helps a mortgage holder in the case of the insured's death or disability. This type of policy will pay the balance of a mortgage in the event of the insured's death, or will help to make the payments on a mortgage if the insured becomes dead or disabled.

M

Mortgage redemption insurance *(Health Insurance/Life Insurance)* — This term can sometimes refer to mortgage insurance. It can also refer to a term policy, the value of which reduces monthly, which is used as mortgage insurance.

Mortgagee *(Property Insurance)* — The person or institution who lends money against the value of a property and receives a mortgage in return.

Mortgagor *(Property Insurance)* — The person who grants a mortgage on a property in exchange for a loan.

Motor truck cargo policy-carriers form *(Property Insurance)* — A form that grants indemnity to the trucker for loss or damage to the property he or she is transporting. By law, truckers must carry a certain amount of this coverage.

Motor truck cargo policy-owners form *(Property Insurance)* — A form that covers a truck owner against the loss of his or her property while it is being transported. This form also covers cargo loss or damage, without regard to who is legally liable for the loss.

Motor vehicle record *(Vehicle Insurance)* — A history of a driver's traffic violations and accidents.

Multi peril crop insurance *(Property Insurance)* — Insurance that covers crop loss due to weather conditions, insects, flood, or other named perils.

Multi peril policies *(General Insurance Terms)* — Policies that provide coverage against multiple perils in one contract.

Multi-disciplinary *(Health Insurance)* — Treatment that requires multiple specialists of different disciplines.

Multiemployer plan *(Pensions)* — A plan in which more than one employer contributes, or a plan required by a collective bargaining agreement.

Multiple employer trust *(Health Insurance)* — A trust comprised of several small employers who work in the same field. This trust is created to purchase group insurance at a lower cost, or establish a self-funded plan.

Multiple employer welfare arrangements *(Health Insurance)* — Funds and trusts financed by the employer to provide medical benefits.

§M§

Multiple funding *(Pensions)* — Using a separate fund as well as insurance cash values to provide retirement benefits.

Multiple indemnity *(Life Insurance)* — A clause stating that the benefits provided by a certain policy will be multiplied by a certain percentage if the peril happens in a specified way; for example, double indemnity on a property insurance policy in the case of arson.

Multiple line law *(General Insurance Terms)* — A state law that makes it legal for the same insurer to write both property and casualty insurance.

Multiple line policy *(General Insurance Terms)* — Any kind of personal or commercial package policy that includes many different coverages.

Multiple location policy *(Property Insurance)* — A policy that covers property owned by one person in more than one location.

Multiple location rating plan *(Property Insurance)* — A plan offered to commercial clients who operate from more than one location, with credits offered that are based on the number of locations. Under this kind of plan, the multiple locations are seen as a reduced hazard, as the assets are spread between these locations.

Multiple option plan *(Health Insurance)* — A plan under which employees can choose between an HMO, PPO, or a major health plan.

Multiple protection insurance *(Liability Insurance)* — A mixture of term life and whole life insurance that pays out a multiple of the face value during the term policy's period, and then turns into a whole life policy after the term is over. The period known as the "multiple protection period" is the time during which both policies are in effect.

Mutual atomic energy reinsurance pool *(Liability Insurance)* — A group of mutual insurance companies who provide reinsurance of liability policies that cover private nuclear energy reactors. This type of insurance can only be written by a pool.

Mutual benefit association *(General Insurance Terms)* — An association that offers benefits to its members. Under the benefit plan, no regular premiums are paid. Instead, assessments are made with each loss as it occurs.

Mutual fund *(General Insurance Terms)* — An insurance company that brings in funds by selling its stock to the public. This money is then invested in other securities, and the value of the mutual fund changes based on the value of the investments in the portfolio. There can be two kinds: an open-end mutual fund, in which shares can be sold at any point, and closed-end, in which only the amount of shares originally authorized may be sold.

Mutual insurer *(General Insurance Terms)* — An incorporated insurer that does not have incorporated capital belonging to the policyholders. These companies do still provide the policyholders with dividends.

Mutual insurer policy *(General Insurance Terms)* — Coverage written by an insurer that does not have incorporated capital belonging to the policyholders, although it is an incorporated insurer.

Mutualization *(General Insurance Terms)* — Having an insurer purchase stock and retire it. This is done to convert a stock insurer to a mutual insurer.

Mysterious disappearance *(Criminal)* — A term used to give broader coverage than named perils like robbery. This term refers to a property disappearance that cannot be explained.

M

N

Name position bond *(Criminal)* — A fidelity bond that covers the insured in the event of a loss caused by fraud on the part of an employee working in a position listed in the bond.

Name schedule bond *(Criminal)* — A fidelity bond similar to the name position bond. The insured is covered in the event of a loss caused by dishonesty of an employee specifically named in the bond.

Named insured *(General Insurance Terms)* — The insured listed in the policy, whether a person or entity. People not named in the policy may still be protected in certain circumstances. For example, if they are passengers in an insured car and are harmed in an accident, certain kinds of policies may cover them.

Named non-owner policy *(Vehicle Insurance)* — A policy written for a person who drives a car he or she does not own; for example, a borrowed or rented car.

Named perils *(Property Insurance)* — The potential causes of loss that are covered on an insured property.

National Association of Health Underwriters *(Health Insurance)* — An association of professionals that service health care needs, including brokers, agents, and consultants. The association aims to offer education and support to its members, so that they may meet the health and retirement requirements of all Americans.

National Association of Independent Insurers *(General Insurance Terms)* — An association that disseminates information about insurance law and legislation

National health insurance *(Health Insurance)* — A system of insurance benefits established by a federal government to cover all or almost all of the citizens of the country. These systems are entirely or partially funded with tax money. The United States is developing a program like this.

National Safety Council *(General Insurance Terms)* — An organization charged with distributing safety education materials. This nonprofit organization was established by U.S. Congress in 1913.

Natural death *(General Insurance Terms)* — Death due to natural causes, defined as any cause other than accident or homicide.

Natural premium *(Life Insurance)* — The mortality cost of life insurance for one year.

Negligence *(General Insurance Terms/Legal Terminology)* — A failure to exercise the amount of care an ordinary person would use in a certain circumstance.

Net amount at risk *(Liability Insurance)* — The difference between the face value of the policy and the reserve accumulated under that policy.

Net cost *(General Insurance Terms)* — The total premiums paid minus their cash value and any dividends generated by the policy as of the time the difference is being calculated. Insurers who supply life insurance policies usually make comparisons of net cost every ten or 20 years.

Net increase *(Life Insurance)* — The amount of new policies written and renewed less the amount of policies lapsed or cancelled. This calculation helps the insurer to determine the total amount of business the insurer has in force during a specific time frame.

Net interest earned *(General Insurance terms)* — The average amount of interest earned on an insurer's investments after investment expense and before income taxes.

Net level premium *(Life Insurance)* — The pure cost of a life insurance policy through the term of the policy divided by the number of years it is in force.

Net level premium reserve *(Health Insurance/Life Insurance)* — The reserve an insurer must maintain to pay net level policies in their later years.

Net line *(General Insurance Terms/Reinsurance)* — In reinsurance, this term refers to the amount of insurance retained by the original insurer on a particular risk in a surplus treaty. This term can also be used to refer to the maximum amount of loss an insurer will be exposed to unless they seek reinsurance.

Net loss *(General Insurance Terms)* — The portion of a loss the insurer is left with after all reinsurance, salvage, or subrogation coverage.

Net premium *(General Insurance Terms)* — A general term that can have many different meanings. This term can refer to a premium with the amount of the agent's commission deducted. This term can also mean the portion of the premium required to pay expected future losses. This term can also refer to the premium amount with the amount of dividends that have been appointed to pay part of the premium deducted.

Net quick assets *(Surety)* — Also referred to as the working capital. To be bonded, a contractor needs to have sufficient working capital, which is calculated as the difference between current allowable assets and current changeable liabilities.

Net rate *(Liability Insurance)* — The amount of a premium after the dividends appointed to pay it have been deducted. This term can also refer to the rate found in a rate book for a nonparticipating policy.

Net retention *(General Insurance Terms)* — The insurance a ceding company keeps and does not reinsure.

Net worth *(Surety)* — The margin by which a company's assets exceed their liabilities.

Network model HMO *(Health Insurance)* — An HMO model that contracts with multiple physician groups. The physician groups are free to provide care for other individuals not covered by the HMO.

New for old *(General Insurance Terms)* — Purchasing new parts to replace old or damaged parts instead of repairing the old ones.

New York standard fire policy *(Property Insurance)* — A basic contract for fire insurance that was widely used in almost all states. The policy covered losses due to fire, as well as lightening, and was a predecessor to modern forms. This policy is no longer widely used, but still exists in some states.

Newly acquired autos *(Vehicle Insurance)* — A newly purchased vehicle, which the insured must notify the insurer about within 30 days of purchase. Vehicles purchased during the term of the policy receive some coverage automatically under the policy.

Newspaper policy *(Health Insurance)* — A limited health insurance policy that is sold by newspaper advertisements with the aim of increasing circulation.

No-fault insurance *(Vehicle Insurance)* — Insurance that permits the injured party in an automobile accident to file claims to his or her insurance company, without regard to who caused the accident. This type of insurance is legally mandated in many states.

Nominal damages *(Legal Terminology)* — In a case which damages have not been proven, the plaintiff may be awarded a small sum. This is done to verify the plaintiffs' legal rights.

Nonadmitted assets *(General Insurance Terms)* — Assets not qualified to be listed on the insurance statements because they do not meet state requirements. These can include furniture or fixtures.

Nonadmitted insurer *(General Insurance Terms)* — An insurer who is not able to do business in a certain jurisdiction, as he or she does not have the proper license.

Nonadmitted reinsurance *(Reinsurance)* — Reinsurance that is not credited on the ceding company's annual statement because the reinsurer is not properly licensed in the jurisdiction where the business was conducted.

Nonassessable policy *(General Insurance Policy)* — A policy wherein extra premiums cannot be added. The premium amount is set.

Nonassignable *(General Insurance Policy)* — A policy that cannot be assigned to a third party by the owner. The majority of policies are nonassignable.

Noncancellable *(Health Insurance)* — A policy contract that specifies that the insured may continue coverage by paying the premiums for a specific time frame. During the same time frame, the insurer is prohibited from making changes. The premiums on this type of policy cannot be changed during the term.

Nonconcurrency *(Property Insurance)* — When several policies that cover the same property against the same perils do not provide the same amount of coverage. This usually causes the insured to be underinsured should a loss occur.

Nonconfining sickness *(Health Insurance)* — An illness that does not force the insured to remain indoors.

Noncontributory *(Health Insurance/Life Insurance)* — A form of insurance wherein the employer pays the full premium and the employee is not required to contribute at all.

Noncontributory retirement plan *(Pensions)* — A retirement plan wherein the employer pays the full premium amount.

Noncupative will *(Estate)* — A will spoken by a person very close to dying, in the presence of witnesses.

Non-disabling injury *(Health Insurance)* — A lesser injury that may be eligible for a small benefit; for example, a month's payment of disability benefits. This type of injury is less severe than a total or partial disability.

Non-disabling injury rider *(Health Insurance)* — A rider found in disability income policies that does not pay a benefit. Instead, it allows for the payment of medical costs that are sustained due to an injury that does not cause a total disability.

Nonduplicaion of benefits *(Health Insurance)* — Also called coordination of benefits. A clause found in certain policies stating that benefits will not cover losses already being covered by another party.

Nonforfeitable benefit *(Pensions)* — A pension plan benefit that belongs to the insured and cannot be lost.

Nonforfeiture values *(Life Insurance)* — The parts of a policy that cannot be denied to the policyholder, even if he or she stops paying the premiums. The policyholder may choose either the paid up surrender value, the cash surrender value, the loan value, and the extended term insurance value. If he or she does not choose one of these, there is one specified in the contract that will take effect.

Noninsurable risk *(General Insurance Terms)* — A risk that cannot be insured, either because the probability of a loss is too high, or because it cannot be measured actuarially.

Noninsurance *(General Insurance Terms)* — A total lack of financial preparation for potential losses.

Nonmedical *(Health Insurance/Life Insurance)* — A policy written without the insured submitting to a medical examination. The insured's statement of health is deemed sufficient.

Non-occupational policy *(Health Insurance)* — A policy that does not cover injuries sustained while at work, because those injuries are covered by workers compensation.

Nonowned auto *(Vehicle Insurance)* — A vehicle that has been rented, leased, or borrowed and is used for business purposes

Nonparticipating *(General Insurance Terms)* — A type of policy that does not pay dividends to the policy holder because the contract does not require them to be.

Nonparticipating provider *(Health Insurance)* — A provider who is not authorized to participate in Medicare. This term can also refer to a provider who is not yet contracted with a health plan.

Nonparticipating provider indemnity benefits *(Health Insurance)* — A type of coverage wherein reimbursement is provided for medical services performed by nonparticipating medical providers.

Nonprofit insurers *(Health Insurance)* — Insurers that are established according to state laws with the purpose of supplying medical expense reimbursement coverage.

Nonqualified plan *(Pensions)* — An employee benefit plan that does not need to be filed with the IRS and does not offer a tax deduction in exchange for contributions. Under this type of plan, the employer may discriminate with regard to who can receive coverage, and certain employees can be allocated more benefits than others.

Nonrenewal *(General Insurance Terms)* — Refusal on the part of either the insurer or the insured to renew coverage. This may be done by either party on the expiration date or the policy's anniversary.

Nonresident agent *(General Insurance Terms)* — An agent who is licensed to sell insurance in a state other than the one he lives in.

Nonvalued policy *(General Insurance Terms)* — A policy that is written without specifying an amount to be paid out in the case of a loss.

Noon clause *(Property Insurance)* — A clause stating that coverage begins at noon. This clause is not often found anymore, and most policies are effective as of 12:01 a.m.

Normal retirement *(Pensions)* — Retirement taken at the time the pension plan has deemed normal.

Normal retirement benefit *(Pensions)* — The employee's early retirement benefit or the benefit to be paid upon normal retirement, whichever amount is greater. The value of these amounts does not take in to account the medical or disability benefits provided.

Not otherwise classified (NOC) *(Liability Insurance/ Workers Compensation)* — A term used by workers compensation rating manuals or liability manuals. Listings that are followed by the abbreviation NOC are to be used only if the insured cannot be otherwise classified.

Not taken *(General Insurance Terms)* — A policy that has been applied for and issued to the possible insured but rejected and not taken or paid for.

N

Notice of cancellation *(General Insurance Terms)* — Written notification of imminent cancellation from either party. Either the insured is requesting cancellation from the insurer, or the insurer is notifying the insured of its intent to cancel the coverage.

Notice of loss *(General Insurance Terms)* — Notice sent to an insurer informing them that a loss has occurred. How and when this notice must take place is usually specified in the policy.

Notice to company *(General Insurance Terms)* — A notification, in written form, sent to the insurer, informing them of an event upon which a claim will be based.

Nuisance value *(General Insurance Terms)* — An amount the insurer pays to settle a claim because they are ready to be done with it, not because the claim is valid.

Numerical rating *(Life Insurance)* — A way of establishing the rate that will be charged for a substandard insured. The standard risk is a 100. Injuries or other impairments are each given a value to be added to 100. The resulting total indicates which table will be used to determine the policy rate.

Nurse fees *(Health Insurance)* — A clause that allows for the reimbursement of amounts paid to nurses who are not employed by a hospital.

Nursing home *(Health Insurance)* — Also called a long-term nursing facility. A licensed center that provides care to those unable to care for themselves or who have a chronic illness.

N

O

Obligee *(Surety)* — A term used to mean the person who is protected by a bond. Comparable to the insured in an insurance policy.

Obligor *(Surety)* — Also called the principal. The person who is bound by an obligation.

Occupancy *(Property Insurance)* — The use of a property. A property's use can affect the rate assigned to the policy.

Occupational accident *(General Insurance Terms)* — An accident caused by a person's employment, or that takes place while doing one's job.

Occupational disease *(Health Insurance)* — A disease caused by exposure to the conditions that one works in, or that occurs as a result of a job.

Occupational hazard *(General Insurance Terms)* — A condition inherent to an occupation that augments the chance of sickness, accident, or death.

Occupational manual *(General Insurance Terms)* — A book that lists classifications of occupations.

Occupational Safety and Health Act (OSHA) *(General Insurance Terms)* — A federal statute that creates safety and health requirements nationwide. This act is enforced by the Labor Department, through safety inspectors, and keeps records of injury statistics.

Occurrence *(General Insurance Terms)* — An incident that causes an insured loss. This is considered different than an accident, because an occurrence does not have to be sudden and unexpected. An occurrence can also be the result of repeated exposure to a certain condition, as long as it is not intentional or predicted by the insured.

Occurrence coverage *(Liability Insurance)* — A form that offers liability coverage for loss that occurs within the policy's term, no matter when the actual claim is made.

Odds *(General Insurance Terms)* — The likely chance that a particular incidence will occur within a statistical sample. This can be expressed as a decimal fraction of total occurrences or as a ratio to the likely number of nonoccurences.

Off premises *(Property Insurance)* — A property insurance clause that extends coverage beyond the location detailed in the policy. This coverage is usually only a percentage of the total coverage.

Offer *(General Insurance Terms)* — The conditions of a contract offered by one party to the other. In life insurance, the initial premium plus the completed application is considered an offer. In property insurance, just the application is considered the offer.

Offeree *(General Insurance Terms)* — The person to whom an offer is extended.

Offeror *(General Insurance Terms)* — A person who makes an offer.

Office burglary and robbery policy *(Criminal)* — A policy created for offices that covers equipment and supplies against crime. Under this policy, the insured must purchase a package of crime coverages, which have a low limit.

Office visit *(Health Insurance)* — Services that are provided by the physician in office.

Officers and directors liability insurance *(Liability Insurance)* — Insurance that covers officers and directors of a company against harm done to the company due to their negligence.

Offset rider *(Health Insurance)* — A rider found in a health insurance policy that reduces benefits by a fraction of the social security benefits the insured receives.

Old age survivors disability and health insurance (OASDHI) *(General Insurance Terms)* — A system established by the Social Security Act in 1935. The OASDHI provides benefits for the elderly, disabled workers, and surviving dependents.

Old line *(Life Insurance)* — A term usually used to refer to a non-fraternal insurer operating on the basis of a legal reserve.

Omnibus Budget Reconciliation Act *(Health Insurance)* — A federal law that extends COBRA continuation for those who are considered disabled or were disabled at the time of qualification. Under this law, group health coverage is extended from 18 months to 29 months.

Omnibus clause *(General Insurance Terms)* — A stipulation that extends the coverage to other people not specifically named in the contract, due to its definition of insured.

Omnibus risk *(Property Insurance)* — A building that has several tenants who conduct different businesses.

Open access *(Health Insurance)* — A concept that allows the insured to see another service provider without needing to obtain a referral.

Open debit *(Health Insurance/Life Insurance)* — A debit (territory) that does not currently have an agent.

Open end investment company *(Pensions)* — Also called a mutual fund. An investment company that is run by investment advisers who invest on behalf of shareholders.

Open enrollment period *(Health Insurance)* — The period during which members can choose to fall under an alternate plan, without having to provide proof of insurability.

Open perils *(General Insurance Terms/Property Insurance)* — Insurance that covers loss or property damage caused by any peril except those specifically excluded.

Open policy *(Property Insurance)* — A type of insurance most often used on goods in transit. The contract does not specifically state policy terms or an expiration date, but a certificate of insurance that states the goods to be covered is issued. The contract does specify limits of liability under the coverage it offers. Reports are made monthly and premiums are due at that time.

Open rating *(General Insurance Terms)* — A system wherein the insurer is allowed by the state to use rates that were not previously approved.

Option *(Life Insurance)* — The ways in which a policyholder can choose to receive dividends, death benefits, or nonforfeiture values.

Optional modes of settlement *(Life Insurance)* — The ways in which a beneficiary can receive the pay out of a policy.

Optionally renewable *(Health Insurance)* — A contract the insurer reserves the ability to terminate at the policy's anniversary or the premium due date, but not at any point in between.

Ordinary agency *(Life Insurance)* — An agency that only deals in ordinary life insurance.

Ordinary construction *(Property Insurance)* — A building constructed with floors that sit on wood joists, little protection of stair shafts, and interior finishes that limit the space to which fire can spread.

Ordinary life pension trust *(Pensions)* — A pension plan that gets funding from a trust. This type of pension plan provides death benefits for participating employees through life insurance contracts that are purchased for them. The trust will pay the premium amount on the life insurance policy until the employee retires, then uses the paid up insurance policy's value to purchase retirement benefits.

Ordinary life policy *(Life Insurance)* — A life insurance policy with premiums that are paid for as long as the insured lives.

Ordinary payroll *(Property Insurance)* — The total amount of payroll expenses for all the employees of an insured business. This does not include payroll for executives, contract employees, officers of the company, and department managers. This amount may or may not be included in a business insurance form.

Ordinary register *(Life Insurance)* — A record book that is kept by an agency or insurer that lists data on the ordinary policies in an agent's account.

Other insurance *(General Insurance Terms)* — Other contracts that cover the same property and perils.

Other insurance clause *(General Insurance Terms)* — A clause that details what will be done if another insurance contract covers the same property. This clause is found in most insurance policies, aside from life and health insurance.

Other structures *(Property Insurance)* — Additional structures on the insured's property that are detached from the insured's home by an empty space. These structures may be connected by a fence or power line. Homeowners insurance usually covers these structures; for example, a tool shed or garage.

Out of area *(Health Insurance)* — Treatment provided to the insured outside of the usual service area.

Out of pocket costs *(Health Insurance)* — The money the insured or covered person must pay themselves; for example, a co-payment.

Out of pocket limit *(Health Insurance)* — The highest coinsurance an insured will have to pay. After this amount is paid, the insurer will cover all expenses up to the policy limit.

Outage insurance *(Property Insurance)* — Insurance that covers lost earnings due to machinery failure due to an insured peril that damages the insured's premises.

Outcomes measurement *(Health Insurance)* — A way of measuring the treatment provided to a patient and the patient's responses to each treatment.

Outline of coverage *(Health Insurance/Life Insurance)* — A short explanation of benefits, coverage, exclusions, and premiums that is given to an applicant for insurance. This serves only as a summary and does not exclude all of the information the policy contract does.

Out-of-area *(Health Insurance)* — Treatment provided outside of the usual geographic coverage area.

Out-of-pocket costs *(Health Insurance)* — The costs the insured must pay; for example, deductible or prescription medication costs.

Out-of-pocket limit *(Health Insurance)* — The limit on coinsurance the patient will have to pay before all expenses will be paid by the insurer, up to the policy limit.

Outpatient *(Health Insurance)* — A patient who does not reside in or have a bed in the hospital where he or she receives treatment.

Outstanding premiums *(General Insurance Terms)* — Premiums that are currently due but have not yet been paid.

Over insured *(General Insurance Terms)* — When an individual has coverage for more than the value of item that is insured. This term can also refer to an individual who has so much insurance it poses a moral hazard; for example, a person who has so much disability insurance that they exaggerate symptoms to linger on disability status.

Over-the-counter drugs *(General Insurance Terms)* — Drugs that may be purchased without a prescription from a medical professional.

Overage insurance *(Health Insurance)* — Health insurance issued to an insured over the age of 65, which is the usual limit.

Overhead expense insurance *(Health Insurance)* — Disability insurance for business owners. In the event that the business owner becomes disabled, this insurance will pay rent, bills such as utilities, and salaries for the business employees.

Overlapping insurance *(General Insurance Terms)* — Insurance from at least two insurers that duplicates the coverage of some risks.

Overlie *(General Insurance Terms)* — The amount of insurance or reinsurance that exceeds the insurer or reinsurer's usual capacity. This term can also refer to an insurer or reinsurer's commitment over and above the usual capacity.

Overriding commission *(General Insurance Terms)* — A commission paid to an agent or broker on business sold by subagents in his or her territory. This term can also refer to an amount paid to a ceding company in addition to the acquisition cost to compensate for overhead expenses.

Owners and contractors protective liability policy *(Liability Insurance)* — Also called independent contractors insurance. Insurance that covers the insured in the case of a loss stemming from contractor or subcontractor negligence.

Owners, landlords, and tenants liability insurance *(Liability Insurance)* — A form of liability insurance intended to cover places where the public often visit. This form provides coverage against liability arising from bodily injury or property damage caused by the owner's negligence. The commercial general liability coverage form has mostly replaced this form.

Ownership *(Life Insurance)* — Denotes the person who controls all of the benefits and privileges associated with a life insurance policy. The title of owner may belong to someone other than the insured and may be transferred by the owner's written request.

Ownership of expirations *(General Insurance Terms)* — An agreement made with an insurer that states that some pieces of information will not be shared with any agent or broker other than the one who originated the policy. This is usually a property or liability form.

Ownership provision *(Life Insurance)* — A provision that states that a policy may be owned by a different person than the one insured.

Package policy *(General Insurance Terms)* — An insurance policy that includes more than two different kinds of coverage; for example, personal and commercial.

Paid business *(Health Insurance/Life Insurance)* — An insurance policy for which the prospective insured has filled out and signed the application, submitted a premium payment, and undergone the medical exam.

Paid claims *(Health Insurance)* — Under a health plan, the amounts paid to health care providers.

Paid claims loss ratio *(Health Insurance)* — A ratio calculated as paid claims divided by total premiums.

Paid for *(General Insurance Terms)* — Insurance for which the premium has been paid.

Paid losses *(General Insurance Terms)* — The amount paid out in losses during a particular time frame.

Paid-up insurance *(Life Insurance)* — An insurance policy with all the premiums paid and no amount due that has not yet matured.

Pair and set clause *(Property Insurance)* — A provision stating that if one-half of a pair or part of a set is lost or damaged, a reasonable and fair percentage of the value of both will be assessed. The insurer is not required to pay for the total value of the whole set.

Parasol policy *(Liability Insurance)* — The Difference in Conditions policy by another name. A contract separate from the existing policy that complements or increases the property insurance, so that the property is now protected from all risks, minus some exclusions.

Parcel post insurance *(Property Insurance)* — Insurance coverage, provided by either a private company or the United States Post Office, for items or parcels under the care of the United States Postal Service. These items are usually insured against damage or loss.

Parent company *(General Insurance Terms)* — The oldest company out of a group of insurers.

Parol *(Legal Terminology)* — A term used in legal proceedings to designate an oral statement, as opposed to a written one.

Parol evidence rule *(Legal Terminology)* — A rule stating that a written agreement or contract cannot be changed by a verbal agreement. This rule is based on the idea that contracts should include all facts and modifications to the existing agreements.

Partial disability *(Health Insurance)* — A disability that occurs as a result of injury or illness. Each insurance policy defines this term differently, but generally this term refers to a disability that prevents the insured from completing all of the tasks that his or her occupation requires. The insured is still capable of performing some of these tasks.

Partial hospitalization services *(Health Insurance)* — Outpatient treatment provided to mental health or substance abuse patients as a substitute for or continuation of inpatient treatment.

Partial loss *(General Insurance Terms)* — A loss that does not totally devalue or ruin the insured's property.

Participant *(General Insurance Terms)* — An individual who is eligible to receive benefits from a health, life, or pension plan.

Participating *(General Insurance Terms)* — A policy that pays dividends to the policy owner. This term can also refer to insurance that pays a portion of the loss, along with other insurance coverage that applies to the same risk.

P

Participating provider *(Health Insurance)* — A medical provider approved to participate in the Medicare program. These providers are paid directly by carriers.

Participation *(Health Insurance)* — The total number of employees enrolled in a plan as compared to the total number of employees eligible for coverage.

Particular average *(Property Insurance)* — A partial loss caused by a form of water transportation, which the property owner must bear the cost of entirely.

Partnership insurance *(Life Insurance/Health Insurance)* — Insurance sold to a partnership. Most often, this insurance is purchased to aid the business in continuing to operate in case of the death or dismemberment of one partner. There are two plans most often used in partnership insurance. Under a cross purchase plan, each of the partners purchases life insurance on the other, with themselves listed as the beneficiary. If one partner dies, the surviving partner uses the payout of the life insurance to purchase the deceased partner's interest in the company. This type of plan works best for a company with only two partners, while an entity plan works better for a team with multiple partners. Under an entity plan, the partnership purchases the life insurance policies on each partner, and is the beneficiary on each policy. Should one partner die, the partnership uses the insurance payout to buy the deceased person's interest.

Party in interest *(Pensions)* — Any individual involved in the actual services provided by or the establishing of an employee policy; for example, the medical professionals who provide service under the plan, or the person at the employer's office who establishes the plan.

Past service benefit *(Pensions)* — Credit given for time an employee worked prior to a pension or other retirement plan being instituted.

Past service liability *(Pensions)* — The starting value of a pension plan made up of annuity credits that are vested before the effective date.

Paul vs. Virginia *(General Insurance Terms)* — A decision made by the United States Supreme Court in 1869; the court found that insurance is not considered commerce and therefore not regulated by the federal government. This ruling was reversed in 1944 by the ruling made in the Southeastern Underwriters Association case.

Payback period *(General Insurance Terms)* — The length of time it takes for an investment to make the original amount invested. For example, if a $500 investment generates a return of $100 every year, the payback period of that investment is five years.

Payee *(General Insurance Terms)* — A person receiving money.

Paymaster robbery insurance *(Criminal)* — Insurance that covers the loss of money intended for payroll due to a robbery perpetuated by the appointed custodian.

Payment bond *(Surety)* — A bond guaranteeing that a contractor will provide and pay for the labor and materials used on a project. This is done to save the property owner from being liable for the contractor's failure to payment.

P

Payor benefit *(Liability Insurance)* — A provision usually found in juvenile policies. This provision states that if the person responsible for paying the premiums, such as the child's parent, becomes disabled or dies before the child legally becomes an adult, the rest of the premiums are waived.

Payroll audit *(Liability Insurance/Workers Compensation)* — An examination conducted by a representative of the insurance company. This is done to establish the amount of the last premium due for the most recent policy year.

Payroll deduction insurance *(Life Insurance)* — When an employee has authorized his or her employer to deduct insurance premiums from his or her paycheck. The employer then sends the amount deducted on to the insurer periodically.

Peak season endorsement *(Property Insurance)* — This endorsement offers more coverage on the insured inventory during peak seasons. The dates this increased coverage applies are listed in the endorsement.

Peer review *(Health Insurance)* — A review of medical treatment, conducted by a medical staff with equal training to those who provided the care.

Peer review organization *(Health Insurance)* — Physicians hired by the federal government to review the service provided to Medicare subscriber by the Medicare approved facilities.

Penalty *(Surety)* — The maximum value the insurance company is liable for, according to a Fidelity Bond.

Pension plan *(Pensions)* — A type of retirement plan designed to pay employees and their spouses with a monthly income for the rest of their lives, after they have met age and service requirements. Death and disability benefits are also usually part of the plan. Under the Employee Retirement Income Security Act, the pension plan must supply the retired person with an income for the remainder of his or her life, and half that to a surviving spouse.

Pension trust fund *(Pensions)* — A fund comprised of money intended pay for pension benefits. This money is contributed by the employer and the employee.

Per capita *(Life Insurance)* — A form of sharing a beneficiary's portion in an estate equally between every one of their heirs.

Per cause deductible *(Health Insurance)* — A requirement stating that benefits are only paid after the deductible for each incident is met.

Per diem business interruption *(Property Insurance)* — A type of business interruption policy. If the everyday business is interrupted due to a covered cause, this type of policy will pay a specified amount for each day that the business is unable to open.

Per risk excess reinsurance *(Reinsurance)* — A kind of reinsurance wherein the insurer pays the loss up to a stated limit, and the reinsurer pays the rest of the loss up to the limit.

Per stirpes *(Life Insurance)* — The sharing of property between multiple beneficiaries. If the insured should outlive one of these beneficiaries, the deceased beneficiary's heir shall inherit the beneficiary's share of the property.

P

Percentage participation *(Health Insurance)* — A provision stating that the insurer and the insured will pay specified portions of any losses, which they have agreed to in the contract.

Percentage test *(Pensions)* — A test used to establish whether a qualified plan will benefit 70 percent of the employees on the lower end of the pay scale.

Performance bond *(Surety)* — A bond issued to guarantee a contract will be performed properly.

Peril *(General Insurance Terms)* — A potential cause of loss.

Period of restoration *(Property Insurance)* — The term of a business income coverage policy payout. This time frame starts on the date the loss that interrupts business occurs and ends on the date that the property should be fixed.

Permanent and total disability *(Health Insurance)* — A disability the insured does not recover from. This designation is usually given to the disability after six months.

Permanent life insurance *(Life Insurance)* — A broad term for any kind of life insurance other than group or term policies.

Permanent partial disability *(Health Insurance/Workers Compensation)* — A disability the insured is impaired by, but not totally incapacitated by. The insured is still able to work in some capacity.

Permanent total disability *(Health Insurance)* — A disability that makes it impossible for the insured to work for the rest of his or her life.

Permit bond *(Surety)* — A bond that promises the person issued a permit will follow the laws that govern the activity for which the permit was issued.

Persistency *(Life Insurance)* — A factor important in underwriting; this term refers to the chance of the insurer's business not lapsing or being replaced by another insurer's coverage.

Personal assets *(General Insurance Terms)* — Items of value and cash belonging to the insured; for example, cars, real estate, and jewelry.

Personal auto policy *(Vehicle Insurance)* — The most commonly sold auto insurance policy. This type of policy is a modified version of the family auto insurance policy.

Personal effect floater *(Property Insurance)* — This can be a specified risk or open peril policy that covers the personal property carried by the insured while he or she is traveling.

Personal injury *(Liability Injury)* — A non-bodily injury that arises due to one of the following causes: libel, slander, false arrest, wrongful eviction, or violation of right to privacy.

Personal injury protection *(Vehicle Insurance)* — A term that refers to no-fault benefits in certain states, namely those that require vehicle insurance or those with voluntary no-fault insurance. This type of benefit usually includes loss of income, medical costs, and accidental death.

Personal liability supplement *(Liability Insurance)* — A form, usually attached to a dwelling policy, that provides personal liability coverage.

Personal lines *(General Insurance Terms)* — A general term that refers to any insurance that covers individuals or families; for example, health insurance or homeowners insurance.

Personal property *(Property Insurance)* — Any items belonging to the insured, outside of real estate. These items are usually best protected under a homeowners insurance policy. This term includes, but is not limited to, televisions, jewelry, cameras, articles of clothing, and furniture. The personal property of a business is usually protected by a commercial form.

Personal property floater *(Property Insurance)* — A policy that covers all of the insured's property in any location, and regardless of where the insured is at the time of loss. This is an all perils coverage that excludes certain circumstances, such as war or nuclear disaster.

Personal property of others *(General Insurance Terms)* — Property that does not belong to the insured named in the contract. This term excludes real estate. This type of property left in the insured's care and custody may be covered under homeowners or commercial property.

Personal surety *(Surety)* — A sole individual who guarantees the acts of another person , as opposed to an insurer or other corporate entity which acts in this capacity.

Personalty *(Legal Terminology)* — The items of property that can be moved, unlike real property, which remains in the same location.

Pharmacy and therapeutics committee *(Health Insurance)* — Sometimes referred to as a P&T committee. A committee comprised of doctors who provide advice to the health plan regarding prescription drugs and their use.

P.S. 58 charges *(Liability Insurance)* — Under certain plans, such as the split dollar plan, the taxable economic benefit available to an employee is equal to the P.S. 58 charges minus the contributions they have made. The amount of P.S. 58 charges is determined by a table generated by the IRS showing the cost of pure death protection.

Physical damage *(General Insurance Terms/Vehicle Insurance)* — A general term for any damage done to property. In a vehicle insurance policy, this term can refer to damage done to a vehicle by collision, theft, or other insured peril.

Physical exam and autopsy *(Health Insurance)* — A clause that is standard in most health insurance policies. This clause stipulates that the insurer may examine the insured if a claim is pending, at the insurer's expense. If the insured is dead, the insurer is permitted to conduct an autopsy.

Physical hazard *(General Insurance Terms)* — A hazard caused by the features of the risk, whether they be structural or operational.

Physician contingency reserve *(Health Insurance)* — A stored amount of funds made up of money deducted from a claim. Prior to paying the doctor, this amount is kept by the health plan. This is done to motivate the physician to provide appropriate care. The amount kept is sometimes paid to the physician later on or it may be used toward claims that must be paid.

Physicians and surgeons' equipment form *(Property Insurance)* — Form that provides coverage for doctors' and dentists' property. Usually covers office equipment, supplies, and furnishings.

Physicians and surgeons professional liability insurance *(Liability Insurance)* — Insurance that covers physicians and surgeons in the case of a malpractice lawsuit or other legal action stemming from the accusation of malpractice.

Physician's current procedural terminology (CPT) *(Health Insurance)* — A manual created by the American Medical Association used to as the standard for detailing medical procedures and other services performed by physicians.

Pilferage *(General Insurance Terms)* — A term that is most often seen in marine insurance forms, used to refer to theft of items of little worth.

Place of service *(Health Insurance)* — The location at which a medical service is provided; for example, a hospital or physicians office.

Plain language laws *(Legal Terminology)* — A state law mandating that laws be written in easy-to-understand language. More complicated terms are only used if a simple term cannot be substituted without confusing the law's meaning.

P

Plan sponsor *(Pensions)* — The organization that establishes a retirement plan; for example, an employer.

Plan year *(Pensions)* — The 12-month period during which plan records are kept on file, whether a calendar year or fiscal year.

Pluvious insurance *(Property Insurance)* — Another term for rain insurance. Insurance that covers losses stemming from an event held outside being cancelled due to rain.

Point of service plan *(Health Insurance)* — A plan wherein the patient can choose a provider whether participating or non-participating.

Policy *(General Insurance Terms)* — A term referring to the contract that begins insurance coverage and any attached forms.

Policy anniversary *(General Insurance Terms)* — The anniversary of the date a policy began. This information is usually listed within the policy's declarations page.

Policy dividend *(General Insurance Terms)* — A dividend paid to the policy holder, made up of a fraction of the premium he or she has paid. It is intended to signify the disparity between the gross premium amount and the actual cost of the policy.

Policy fee *(Life Insurance)* — A now-defunct practice wherein a fee was assessed along with the first premium. This was done to offset initial costs. This term can also refer to a flat rate charge that remains the same regardless of the policy amount. This is used as a kind of quantity discount.

Policy loan *(Life Insurance)* — A loan in the amount of the cash value of a policy. This loan is made by the insurer and uses the policy as collateral.

Policy period *(General Insurance Terms)* — The amount of time during which the policy is valid.

Policy proceeds *(Life Insurance)* — The actual amount paid out by the insurer, either due to death or maturity of the policy. This amount includes dividends on the deposit that have not yet been paid and any extra insurance purchased with the dividend amounts.

Policy reserve *(Life Insurance)* — A reserve created by virtue of the concept that all policies merit a portion of the pro rate reserve.

Policy summary *(Life Insurance)* — A summary of the terms of a life insurance policy, including the conditions, coverage limitations, and premiums. Depending on the laws in the particular location, the policy summary may be required to be issued to potential policyholders with every transaction. The policy summary also includes information on the cost of the policy, such as the premium amounts, and information on the benefit, including the amount to be paid upon death.

Policy year *(General Insurance Terms)* — The 12-month period between the policy's anniversary dates.

Policy year experience *(General Insurance Terms)* — A way of measuring the premiums earned and losses experienced in the 12 months of a policy term.

Policyholder *(General Insurance Terms)* — A term used interchangeably with the terms policy owner or insured. The person insured by a policy.

Policyholder's surplus *(General Insurance Terms)* — The amount available for the insurer to use to meet future obligations.

Policyowner *(General Insurance Terms)* — The person who owns a policy. This person may or may not be the policyholder.

Policywriting agent *(General Insurance Terms)* — An agent charged with and given license to write policies for an insurer.

Pollution liability coverage form *(Liability Insurance)* — A commercial form that covers clean-up costs associated with pollution.

Pollution liability extension endorsement *(Liability Insurance)* — An endorsement that negates portions of the pollution exclusion.

Portfolio *(General Insurance Terms)* — A term which can refer to all the assets in which a company has invested. This term can also refer to all of the policies in effect and losses unsettled.

Portfolio reinsurance *(Reinsurance)* — Reinsurance wherein the reinsurer takes on a portion of the ceding insurer's entire portfolio. This can be done across all classes or just in one class of coverage. This term can also refer to a transfer of the portfolio of an insured through reinsurance.

Portfolio return *(Reinsurance)* — A portfolio, which was once reinsured before, being reinsured yet again.

Portfolio runoff *(Reinsurance)* — Reinsuring a portfolio until such time as all of the ceded premiums have been paid.

Postdated check plan *(Life Insurance)* — A plan under which premiums are paid via post dated checks for the coming year, which have been given to the insurer. The insurer then presents each check on the date the premium is due.

Postmortem dividend *(Life Insurance)* — A dividend paid out after the insured's death.

Power interruption insurance *(Property Insurance)* — Insurance that covers the insured against losses caused by a power failure caused by the hazards named in the policy.

Power of appointment *(Estate)* — The donee's right to choose the end beneficiary of a property. This right is given to the donee by the donor.

Power of attorney *(General Insurance Terms)* — The power to make legal decisions for another person or entity. This power is given to an individual or corporation in a written agreement. This term can also refer to the legal authority given to the head of an insurance exchange by each insured. The head administrator is then called an attorney in fact.

Power plant insurance *(Property Insurance)* — Insurance that covers a power plant against hazards named in the contract.

Practical nurse *(Heath Insurance)* — A licensed nurse who aids patients in performing everyday tasks; for example, eating, bathing, and moving around. This type of nurse is not able to dispense medicine.

Pre-admission authorization *(Health Insurance)* — An authorization that must be obtained from the insurer before the insured can be hospitalized.

Pre-admission certification *(Health Insurance)* — A certification done to see if the insured should be admitted to the hospital. This certification is based on certain established criteria.

Preauthorization check plan *(Life Insurance)* — A payment plan under which premiums are paid by a monthly pre-authorized bank draft.

Precedent *(Legal Terminology)* — A common law concept under which past cases can be used to prove the case currently being tried.

Precertification authorization *(General Insurance Terms)* — A pre-treatment authorization that must be secured from the insurer. The insured's physician must submit a cost estimate and plan for treatment. This is done to control costs, and also allows the insurer to inform the insured ahead of time which services will be covered and which will be at his or her own expense.

Preemptive right *(General Insurance Terms)* — A right given to current stockholders. The stockholder is able to buy newly issued stock before members of the general public, which assures them the ability to keep the same proportion of ownership.

Preexisting condition *(Health Insurance)* — A condition that the insured already had and was already aware of before the policy's effective date. A health insurance policy may not cover these conditions at all or may only cover them for a pre-determined period of time.

Preferred provider organization (PPO) *(Health Insurance)* — An alternative to an HMO network available under certain health insurance plans. A network of care providers who treat members of a health insurance plan for a pre-determined fee. The insured may be required to pay a small co-payment while the rest of the charge is usually covered by the plan. This type of network is less restrictive than an HMO, as the insured is free to choose a hospital and physician.

Preferred risk *(General Insurance Terms)* — A risk better than the standard risk on which the premium rate was based.

Pre-licensing education requirement *(General Insurance Terms)* — A requirement mandating that any person applying for an insurance license has to finish an education course before he or she can be considered eligible for a license.

Preliminary term *(General Insurance Terms)* — Short-term insurance coverage issued to a policyholder to cover the risk until the date the policyholder wishes to establish at the long-term policy's anniversary date.

Premises *(General Insurance Terms)* — The physical location covered by a policy. This can be a property or a fraction of a property.

Premises and operations liability insurance *(Liability Insurance)* — A subline of general liability insurance. Provides liability coverage for potential hazards to a business operation or the business' premises.

Premises burglary *(Criminal)* — A term used in commercial forms to describe a burglary committed on insured premises. Under some commercial policies, this is considered a separate coverage.

Premises theft-outside robbery coverage form *(Criminal)* — A form that covers a robbery that takes place outside of the insured premises. This form usually does not cover money or securities.

Premium *(General Insurance Terms)* — The amount of payment due for insurance coverage that lasts for a certain time period, usually a month or a year.

Premium adjustment form *(Property Insurance)* — A form under which a premium is made at the beginning of the term as a deposit. Throughout the policy term, reports are made by the insured detailing the potential exposures, and the premium amount is adjusted at the time the report is reviewed or at the end of the policy term.

Premium and dispersion credit plan *(Property Insurance)* — A plan that allocates credits to commercial property policyholders with multiple locations. The credits are awarded because the multiple locations constitute a reduced risk, because the potential losses are divided between them. Other factors that may also result in credits.

Premium discount *(General Insurance Terms)* — A discount given to policyholders that pay premiums for one year in advance. This term can also refer to a discount given in some states to holders of workers compensation or general liability policies. This discount is given because of the reduced expense incurred by the insurer on smaller policies.

Premium load *(Life Insurance)* — Also called a front end load. Refers to the fraction of the premium amount that goes to cover insurer expenses.

Premium loan *(General Insurance Terms)* — A loan provided to the insured by the insurer. The loan is made to pay a premium and the cash value of the insurance policy is the security.

Premium notice *(General Insurance Terms)* — A notice that provides the date a premium will be due.

Premium rate *(General Insurance Terms)* — The cost of insurance, broken down to a per-unit cost.

Premium receipt *(General Insurance Terms)* — A receipt issued to the policyholder by the insurer or the insurer's agent which proves that payment has been received.

Premium receipt book *(Life Insurance)* — A book of receipts kept for the payment of premiums.

Premium refund *(Life Insurance)* — A provision in certain policies that allows the beneficiary to be paid the face amount of the policy as well as the total amount of the premiums paid.

Prepaid legal service plan *(Pensions)* — A benefit that provides legal services to the employees.

Prepayment of premiums *(General Insurance Terms)* — Payment ahead of time for upcoming premiums. This can be done through paying the present value of the premiums right away, or through the interest earned on a deposit.

Prescription medication *(Health Insurance)* — Medication that must be prescribed by a doctor.

Present interest *(Estate)* — The usage and enjoyment of property at the present time.

Present value *(General Insurance Terms)* — The current value of an amount due in the future.

Presumption of agency *(General Insurance Terms)* — An agency relationship that is legally enforceable, although no agreement has been signed. This presumption of a relationship exists when the insurer acts in a way that gives the idea that someone is his or her agent before the agent has truly been accepted by them; for example, by providing that person with materials bearing the company logo for distribution. The insurer may later be legally liable for that person's acts.

Presumptive disability *(Health Insurance)* — A disability assumed to be permanent and total; for example, a disability that entails loss of vision or hearing or the loss of two or more limbs. Policyholders having this type of disability do not have to repeatedly undergo medical examinations to show that their disability continues to impair them.

Pretext interview *(General Insurance Terms)* — An interview wherein one party misrepresents his or her identity, the intent behind his or her questions, or the reason for the interview.

Prevailing charge *(Health Insurance)* — The standard charge for a service in the geographical area where the insured resides. This amount is used by Medicare to determine benefit amounts.

P

Preventive care *(Health Insurance)* — Medical care that seeks to prevent illnesses; for example, yearly mammograms or regular checkups.

Prima facie *(Legal Terminology)* — A term used to describe evidence that is adequate enough to prove a point, unless contradicting evidence is presented.

Primary beneficiary *(Life Insurance)* — The first person delegated to receive benefits or a pay-out from an insurance policy after it becomes due.

Primary care *(Health Insurance)* — Medical care provided by a primary physician.

Primary care network (PCN) *(Health Insurance)* — A network made up of primary care doctors who offer medical care to members of a certain plan.

Primary care physician *(Health Insurance)* — A physician, chosen by the insured, who provides primary medical care, and refers the insured to specialists for other types of care.

Primary coverage *(Health Insurance/General Insurance Terms)* — Coverage that pays claims submitted without waiting for another policy to pay first.

Primary insurance amount (PIA) *(Estate)* — A calculation used to determine the amount of social security benefits.

Primary insurer *(Reinsurance)* — Another term for the ceding company.

Principal *(Surety)* — The company or person who is guaranteed by the surety.

Principal sum *(Health Insurance/Life Insurance)* — The total amount to be paid in the event of an accidental death. In the case of dismemberment, a percentage of the principal sum is usually paid.

Prior approval rating forms *(General Insurance Terms)* — A term that may appear in a policy contract, which indicates that the insurer must receive approval from the state before instituting a rate change.

Prior authorization *(Health Insurance)* — A technique for minimizing costs, wherein benefits are only paid if the medical care has been pre-approved.

Priority *(Reinsurance)* — Another term for retention.

Private carrier *(Property Insurance)* — The opposite of a common carrier. A transportation company that is contractually obligated to only transport goods for certain customers.

Private passenger automobile *(Vehicle Insurance)* — Any kind of automobile used to transport private passengers, including a van, which has been approved for use on public motorways.

Pro rata *(General Insurance Terms)* — This term can refer to the allocation of the payout of an insurance policy between several beneficiaries, in the proportions determined in the contract. It can also refer to the sharing of liability between insurers who have policies that cover the same risk. The liability is normally shared according to the amount each policy represents in relation to the total amount of coverage provided by all policies.

Pro rata cancellation *(General Insurance Terms)* — Cancellation of the insurance contract with the premiums adjusted to reflect the amount of time the contract has been in effect.

Pro rata distribution *(General Insurance Terms)* — A clause stipulating that the insurance policy must pay out to each of the subjects of insurance proportionally according to the value each item holds in relation to all of the property items covered in that form.

Pro rata liability clause *(General Insurance Terms)* — A clause stipulating that any loss will be paid proportionally, according to the amount of coverage it provides in relation to the total amount of coverage provided by all policies taken on the same risk.

Pro rata rate *(General Insurance Terms)* — The rate for a shorter term than the usual contract period.

Pro rata reinsurance *(Reinsurance)* — Any kind of reinsurance under which the reinsurer shares losses and premiums with the ceding company.

Probability *(General Insurance Terms)* — The chance that a certain event will occur, represented as a number.

Probable maximum loss (PML) *(Property Insurance)* — The largest loss that can be expected if all goes as it should, such as smoke detectors working.

Probate *(Legal Terminology)* — The dispensation of a deceased person's assets to his or her creditors, the state, and beneficiaries.

Probate bond *(Surety)* — A bond written to protect the assets being administrated by another person, sometimes mandated by probate court.

Probationary period *(Health Insurance)* — A period during which the insured is not yet covered, though the policy is considered effective.

Proceeds *(Life Insurance)* — A term that usually refers to the face value of a policy, but can mean any amount to be paid out by a policy.

Producer *(General Insurance Terms)* — A term for a person who sells insurance; for example, an agent.

Product recall insurance *(Liability Insurance)* — Insurance that covers the costs involved in recalling defective or possibly defective products made by the insured.

Products and completed operations insurance *(Liability Insurance)* — A subline of general liability coverage for manufacturers, and to a lesser degree, contractors. This coverage protects the insured in the event of claims caused by products they have sold, distributed, produced, or handled. Coverage applies only to products that have been sold and are no longer in the insured's possession, or operations that have been finished by the professional.

Professional corporation *(General Insurance Terms)* — A created unit that works in a field that supplies a professional service; for example, healthcare.

Professional Insurance Agents (PIA) Association *(General Insurance Terms)* — An association comprised of mutual insurance agents.

Professional liability insurance *(Liability Insurance)* — Depending on the industry the insured works in, this term can refer to malpractice insurance or errors and omissions insurance.

P

Professional partnership *(General Insurance Terms)* — Two or more people who work together to provide a public service, such as health care.

Profit and commissions insurance *(Property Insurance)* — A type of insurance for those whose income is dependent on commissions or profits tied to a certain property. This insurance covers loss of income due to damage done on the property the income depends on.

Profit sharing plan *(Pensions)* — A type of plan wherein certain employees of a company share in a portion of the company's profits. This portion of the profits is set aside and may be distributed immediately, or may be distributed at a later date, for example, at retirement, death, or termination. This type of plan may qualify for tax exemptions as outlined in the Internal Revenue code.

Prohibited list *(General Insurance Terms)* — Also known as the undesirable list. A list encompassing the risks that a given insurer will not cover.

Prohibited risk *(General Insurance Terms)* — A type of business an insurer will not write cover.

Promulgate *(General Insurance Terms)* — The steps of publicizing of insurance rates, from development to publishing and then setting them into effect. This term can also refer to the act of publicizing a legal order.

Proof of loss *(General Insurance Terms)* — A statement taken from the insured by the insurer, regarding the details of their loss.

The insurer uses the information gained to determine their liability for the loss.

Property damage liability insurance *(Liability Insurance)* — A coverage usually written in conjunction with a bodily injury liability policy. This insurance covers damage done to another person's property, usually including loss of use.

Property insurance *(Property Insurance)* — Insurance that covers the owner or another person with an interest in a property. The insurance covers the loss of income produced through or because of the property.

Property insurance loss register *(Property Insurance)* — A registry created by the American Insurance Association of losses of $500 or more due to fire. Insurers use this information to determine patterns of losses.

Property other than money and securities *(Criminal)* — A term used in commercial crime policies that refers to tangible property other than money that holds intrinsic value; for example, office furniture or supplies.

Proration of benefits *(Health Insurance)* — An adjustment made to medical benefits due to another policy which provides duplicate coverage.

Prospect *(General Insurance Terms)* — A term used to refer to a potential insured.

Prospecting *(General Insurance Terms)* — A term used to refer to activities that have to do with finding prospects.

Prospective payment system *(Health Insurance)* — A payment system used in conjunction with Part A Medicare. Reimbursement is provided according to the insured or patient's condition at the time of admission to the hospital.

Prospective rating *(General Insurance Terms)* — A way of calculating the rates or premiums for a particular period in the future. This method is based on the losses sustained during a particular period in the past.

Prospective rating plan *(General Insurance Terms)* — A plan used to establish premiums for a particular time frame, based on the losses sustained in the previous time frame.

Prospective reimbursement *(Health Insurance)* — A system of annual reimbursement. Providers are paid based on a previously established rate.

Prospective reserve *(Health Insurance/Life Insurance)* — A reserve that should be enough to pay future claims. The amount calculated takes into account future premiums and interest.

P

Protected risk *(Property Insurance)* — A property found within the territory served by a fire department.

Protection *(General Insurance Terms)* — This term can be used as another word for coverage. It can also be used, for example, to refer to a fire station and other tools for fire fighting found in a particular neighborhood.

Protection and indemnity insurance *(Property Insurance)* — A kind of property insurance coverage usually covering a ship's owner against damage done to the crew or cargo due to negligence on their part.

Protection class *(Property Insurance)* — A rating determined by the Grading Schedule of Cities and Towns. This rating is given based on the level of fire protection.

Prototype plan defined *(Pensions)* — A retirement plan that can be used by an employer for free. This is made possible by the sponsorship of an organization.

Provider *(Health Insurance)* — A person or group of people who provide medical care or services; for example, doctors and nurses.

Provisional rate *(General Insurance Terms)* — A temporary rate that can be adjusted at a later time.

Provisions *(General Insurance Terms)* — Also known as a stipulation. A portion of the contract in which benefits and conditions of the policy are explained.

Proximate cause *(Legal Terminology)* — The cause of a loss, which sets off a chain of events resulting in the damage to the insured person or property.

Public adjuster *(General Insurance Terms)* — An adjuster who works on a fee basis on behalf of an insured.

Public assistance *(General Insurance Terms)* — A system providing welfare services, instituted by the state and federal government. Services are provided to the elderly, disabled people, and low-income families.

Public employee's dishonesty coverage *(Criminal)* — Insurance that covers losses due to employee dishonesty. This coverage usually pertains to the loss of money or securities.

Public law 15 *(General Insurance Terms)* — A law put into force by a Congressional Act passed in 1945. Under this law, insurance is not subject to anti-trust laws on the federal level as long as it is properly regulated at the state level.

Public liability insurance *(Liability Insurance)* — Insurance that covers the insured in the case of legal action brought by members of the public. This insurance covers liability due to bodily injury or property damage.

Public official bond *(Surety)* — A type of surety bond wherein the surety, in this case, the company, guarantees that a public official, which is the principal for the bond's purposes, will do their job and properly manage all funds.

Punitive damages *(Legal Terminology)* — Damages awarded as a form of punishment to the person ordered to pay them. This type of damages is usually awarded because of a negligence, omission, or malicious act on the part of an individual or company. These damages may be covered by a general liability policy.

Pure endowment *(Life Insurance)* — An endowment that is only paid if the designated payee is still living at the end of the predetermined endowment period.

Pure loss cost ratio *(Reinsurance)* — The ratio comprising the reinsurer's losses in relation to the premiums received by the ceding company from the subject.

Pure premium *(General Insurance Terms)* — The fraction of the premium payment that is used pay the probable losses.

Pure risk *(General Insurance Terms)* — A risk that is not beneficial to the insurer, as loss is the only foreseeable outcome.

Pyramiding *(General Insurance Terms)* — A situation, most often found in liability insurance, wherein the limits of liability on several policies apply to the same loss, and in so doing create a "pyramid" of higher amounts of insurance that originally seemed to be available.

P

"Q" schedule *(Life Insurance)* — A schedule filed by an insurer with the state, listing the insurer's business expenses. This listing is required by the New York State Code.

Quadruple indemnity *(Life Insurance)* — A form similar to double indemnity, which covers multiple indemnity.

Qualified Medicare beneficiary *(Health Insurance)* — A person who qualifies for Medicare benefits due to his or her income being under the federal poverty guidelines.

Qualified plan *(Pensions)* — An IRS-approved retirement plan. These plans have do not discriminate as to who can participate, and are tax deductible for the contributer, which is usually the employer.

Qualifying event *(Health Insurance)* — An event that causes the insured's coverage; for example, a death, birth, or job loss.

Qualifying terminal interest property *(Estate)* — A trust, the income of which is paid out to the spouse who survives.

Quality assurance *(Health Insurance)* — The process of reviewing the quality of a product or service and taking measures to improve the quality.

Quantity discount *(Life Insurance)* — A discount given to an individual or corporation upon purchasing a policy with a high face value.

Quarantine benefit *(Health Insurance)* — A benefit paid out upon quarantine enforced by health authority. The benefit compensates for the amount of time lost.

Quasi-contract *(Legal Terminology)* — A legal concept used in situations where an actual written contract does not exist. The concept holds that the sitation must be decided as though a contract did exist.

Quasi-insurance institutions *(General Insurance Terms)* — An institution, usually created by the government, that acts in the same manner that an insurance company usually would.

Quick assets *(General Insurance Terms)* — Assets that can be quickly and easily converted into cash.

Quid pro quo *(General Insurance Terms)* — A general legal term which, translated from the Latin, means "one thing for another." When used in an insurance contract, it can refer to the items of value that must be traded for the contract to be valid.

Quota share insurance *(Property Insurance)* — A kind of property insurance contract that shares the same risks with another policy, according to a predetermined percentage.

Quota share re-insurance *(Reinsurance)* — A kind of pro-rata reinsurance in which the ceding insurer is indemnified for each risk listed in the contract. These risks are given a fixed percentage of loss, and paid for by the same fraction of the premium.

R

Rabbi trust *(Pensions)* — A trust wherein the employee is not taxed because the plan's assets can be claimed by creditors. This name is used because the first of these type of trusts was set up for a rabbi.

Radioactive contamination insurance *(Property Insurance)* — Insurance that covers property that can be exposed to radioactive contamination due to materials on the insured property. This type of exposure is usually excluded from typical property insurance policies. To qualify for this type of policy, the possible radioactivity must not be due to exposure from a nuclear reactor or nuclear fuel.

Radius of operation *(Vehicle Insurance)* — The area within which a vehicle is covered for business purposes.

Railroad protective liability *(Liability Insurance)* — Protective liability insurance that is written for those who operate on or next to the railroad's property. This type of coverage tends to favor the railroad.

Railroad retirement *(Health Insurance)* — A retirement program that provides benefits to railroad workers.

Railroad subrogation waiver clause *(Liability Insurance)* — A provision in a property insurance policy, usually written due to the existence of a sidetrack agreement with the railroad. The clause states that the coctract remains valid despite the agreement the insured has with the railroad waiving subrogation against them.

Railroad travel policy *(Health Insurance)* — An insurance policy, similar to travel accident insurance, which is normally sold at the railroad station.

Rain insurance *(Property Insurance)* — Insurance that covers loss of income due to an outdoor event being cancelled because of rain. To be covered, the rain must usually be at least a certain amount and occur during a specified time frame.

Rate *(General Insurance Terms)* — The cost of a particular insurance unit. To arrive at the premium amount, the rate is multiplid by the amount of insurance units being purchased.

Rate card *(General Insurance Terms)* — A small card distributed to agents and sales representatives by an insurer. The card lists the rates available for various coverages.

Rate discrimination *(General Insurance Terms)* — A practice now made illegal by state insurance laws. The practice involved charging different rates to insureds with the same characteristics.

Rate manual *(General Insurance Terms)* — A manual that contains the rates for coverages, and can contain other items such as guidelines to field underwriting, agent guidelines, and cash forfeiture values.

Rate of natural increase/decrease *(General Insurance Terms)* — A rate that equals to the population increase or decrease, without factoring in migration. It is calculated as the birth rate minus the death rate.

Rated *(Life Insurance)* — A term used to refer to coverage that costs more because of the insured's existing injury.

Rating bureau *(General Insurance Terms)* — An organization that classifies rates and the hazards of certain risks by geographic area.

Rating process *(Health Insurance)* — The process used to establish the rate of premiums for a group, based on the risk that they present. During this process, factors such as sex, age, benefits, and cost to administer are considered.

Ratio test *(Pensions)* — A test of coverage, wherein a certain amount of employees on the lower end of the pay scale who benefit from the plan must equal 70 percent of the employees on the higher end of the pay scale.

Readjustment income *(Life Insurance)* — Income that is necessary for the family of a deceased who was the primary wage earner. This income allows the surviving family members time to readjust their spending habits to suit their new income level.

Realty *(Legal Terminology)* — Also called real property. Property that is not movable, such as land, homes, and other structures.

Reasonable and customary charges *(Health Insurance)* — This term can refer to the amount usually charged by a provider in a certain area for a certain service. It can also refer to the cost approved by Medicare for a certain service.

Reassured *(Reinsurance)* — A term used to refer to a company that obtains reinsurance coverage.

Rebate *(General Insurance Terms)* — An incentive offered to the insured for purchasing the insurance, such as money taken from the agent's commission and given to the insured. This type of incentive is illegal. Reduced premiums or rate adjustments are not considered rebates and are therefore legal.

Recapture *(Reinsurance)* — When a ceding company reclaims business that had previously gone to a reinsurer.

Recidivism *(Health Insurance)* — Within the context of health insurance, this term is used to refer to the frequency with which an insured returns to the hospital for inpatient treatment due to the same ailment.

Recipient *(Health Insurance)* — Any person Medicaid has determined is eligible to receive benefits.

Recipient location *(Property Insurance)* — Under business income coverge, one of the types of properties that may be covered. A location where the insured's business is accepted.

Reciprocal insurance exchange *(General Insurance Terms)* — Unrelated individuals who come together to insure each other. Under this type of arrangement, each person takes on a share of the risk. These individuals are known as subscribers, and the plan is administrated by an attorney in fact.

Reciprocity *(Reinsurance)* — The reciprocal placement of insurance. This is done so that the ceding company gives some of its reinsurance to a reinsurer. The reinsurer is, in turn, able to offer reinsurance.

Recording agent *(Property Insurance)* — A term used for an agent who writes property insurance policies. This term is usually only used in the property insurance business.

Recruiting *(General Insurance Terms)* — A general term for the hiring process used to find new employees. In the insurance business, this term is usually used to refer to the process of hiring agents.

Recurrent disability *(Health Insurance/Life Insurance)* — A disability that stems from the same cause as a previous disability, or a related cause.

Recurring clause *(Health Insurance)* — A clause within a health insurance policy that specifies the time period during which a condition is considered a recurrent disability or considered a different condition.

Red-lining *(Property Insurance)* — A discriminatory practice wherein a risk is deemed uninsurable or charged a higher rate due to its location.

Reduced paid-up insurance *(Life Insurance)* — A policy whose cash value can be used to buy paid-up insurance in the highest amount it can afford.

Reduction *(General Insurance Terms)* — A lessening in the amount of benefits paid out under a certain policy due to a particular condition.

Reduction of risk *(General Insurance Terms)* — One of the major risk management techniques. Taking precautionary measures to reduce the likelihood of a loss, or to reduce the severity of a possible loss; for example, installing a security system.

Referral *(Health Insurance)* — A recommendation by the insured's primary care physician that the insured see another doctor, often a specialist.

Referral provider *(Health Insurance)* — The health care provider, often a specialist of some sort, to whom an insured has been referred.

Refund annuity *(Annuity)* — An annuity that issues a refund to the named beneficiary should the annuitant die before benefits amounting to the same total he or she paid on the policy are drawn.

Refund life annuity *(Annuity)* — An annuity that pays out the same amount paid in by the insured. Installment payments are made to the insured during his or her lifetime, and made to the beneficiary after the insured dies.

Regional office *(General Insurance Terms)* — Also known as a branch office. An office where business for a particular geographic area is handled. This office typically reports back to a home office.

Register *(Life Insurance)* — A method of recording all of the policies charged to a particular debt account.

Registered mail insurance *(Property Insurance)* — Insurance that covers money and securities against loss by the post office when sent by registered mail.

Registered nurse *(Health Insurance)* — A medical professional, licensed to provide nursing care, including distributing medication.

Registered representative *(General Insurance Terms)* — An individual who sells securities to members of the public. To become a registered representative, the individual must meet the requirements set by law.

Regular stock option plan *(Pensions)* — A plan available to company executives, wherein the executive is able to buy stock in the company at a previously named price. If stock is purchased under this option, it is considered compensation to the executive, and is taxed as such.

Regulatory information retrieval service *(General Insurance Terms)* — A database that lists actions taken by state insurance departments against insurers and individuals, such as fines and penalities. This database was developed by the NAIC and the state insurance departments.

Rehabilitation benefits *(Workers Compensation)* — Benefits provided under workers compensation to a person injured in a work-related capacity. These are physical rehabilitation or vocational rehabilitation benefits that attempt to prepare the person to return to work.

R

Rehabilitation clause *(Health Insurance)* — A clause within a health insurance policy that provides help with vocational rehabilitation for the policyholder.

Rehabilitation of insurer *(General Insurance Terms)* — A process completed by a state's insurance department with the intent of restoring a financially troubled insurer to solvency.

Rehearing *(Legal Terminology)* — A second hearing, called to highlight an error made during the first hearing.

Reimbursement *(General Insurance Terms)* — Re-payment of an amount already paid by the insured.

Reinstatement *(Reinsurance)* — Re-effecting a catastrophe reinsurance policy that has already paid out for one loss caused by a catastrophe. This is usually done because of payment of a premium, known as a reinstatement premium.

Reinsurance *(Reinsurance)* — A type of insurance used to keep an insurer from sustaining large losses. An insurer, known as the reinsurer, takes on a risk already covered by another insurer, known as the ceding company. The reinsurer may take on the entire risk or a portion of the risk.

R

Reinsurance assumed *(Reinsurance)* — The premium amount associated with the assumption of reinsurance.

Reinsurance broker *(General Insurance Terms)* — A person who works for the ceding insurers placing his or her risks for reinsurance.

Reinsurance credit *(Reinsurance)* — Credit shown on the annual statement of a ceding insurer for premiums on business ceded to a reinsurer and recoverable losses.

Reinsurance premium *(Reinsurance)* — An amount paid to a reinsurer by the ceding insurer, in exchange for the reinsurance provided.

Reinsurer *(Reinsurance)* — The insurer that assumes the insurance written by another company.

Rejection *(General Insurance Terms)* — A term used for an insurer's refusal to insure a given risk. This term can also be used to describe the insurer's refusal to pay a submitted claim.

Relation of earnings to insurance *(Health Insurance)* — A clause stating that if the insured's disability income exceeds the income he or she earns, upon disability the benefits will be reduced to the appropriate amount and premiums that were paid toward excess coverage will be refunded to the insured.

Relative value schedule *(Health Insurance)* — A schedule of surgical costs and values. This schedule lists the values of procedures, as well as the fee that should be paid for each.

Relative value unit *(Health Insurance)* — A unit used in some schedules that list surgical costs and values. The amount to be paid on these schedules is determined by multiplying this factor by a conversion factor.

Release *(General Insurance Terms)* — The act of discarding or doing away with the claim one person has against another. This term can also be used for the document used to terminate such a claim. For example, a lien release is issued to the owner of a property by a contractor after the contractor has been paid for the work they have done.

Remainder *(Reinsurance)* — The amount of risk left over after deducting the amount the ceding company wishes to keep insuring. This is the amount that needs to be reinsured.

Remand *(Legal Terminology)* — A term most often used in the court of appeals. This term refers to the appellate court's decision to return the case to the court it was originally heard by, where further action will then be determined.

Remittitur *(Legal Terminology)* — The process undertaken by the court to reduce an overly large jury verdict.

Removal *(Property Insurance)* — The act of moving property out of a location to prevent it from being lost. Many property insurance forms will cover damage done to items moved to another location to prevent it from loss stemming from a covered peril.

Renewable term *(Life Insurance)* — Refers to a term life policy that may be renewed without the insured having to provide evidence of insurability.

Renewal *(General Insurance Terms)* — The continuation of in-force status that is caused by the payment of a premium.

Renewal commission *(General Insurance Terms)* — The commission paid based on commissions after the first year's commission.

Renewals *(General Insurance Terms)* — A general term used to refer to any premiums paid toward a renewed policy.

Rental value insurance *(Property Insurance)* — A property insurance form that covers a landlord/owner in the case of loss of rental income due to damage done to the property by an insured peril. This form also covers loss sustained to the rental value of the property.

Replacement *(General Insurance Terms)* — A policy written to take the place of an existing policy.

Replacement cost *(Property Insurance)* — The amount required to replace some property, without factoring in depreciation. This amount reflects the cost to replace property with totally new items.

Replacement cost insurance *(Property Insurance)* — Insurance that pays for losses based on the replacement cost.

Reporting form *(Property Insurance)* — A form used by the insured to send the insurer updates on the value of stocks, furniture, and home improvements. This is most often used by an insured with varying inventory.

Representation *(Legal Terminology)* — A portion of the application signed by a potential insured that states that the applicant has provided the information truthfully, to the best of his or her knowledge.

Representative *(General Insurance Terms)* — A general term used for an agent or salesperson.

Res ipsa loquitur *(Legal Terminology)* — A legal doctrine under which a person is deemed negligent if he or she is found to have had total and sole control over the circumstances of an injury, and

R

the injury was only possible if the individual in question had been negligent.

Rescission *(Legal Terminology)* — The early termination of an insurance policy by the insurer due to the discovery of a material representation by the insured. This term can also refer to the act of repudiating a contract, whether because of someone's failure to perform as expected, or because the contract was signed under false pretenses or duress.

Reserve *(General Insurance Terms)* — The amount kept by the insurer to be able to cover all his or her debts. This term can also refer to an amount earmarked by the insurer for a specific purpose.

Residence employee *(Workers Compensation)* — A person employed to perform household services.

Residence premises *(Liability Insurance)* — The building in which the homeowners insurance policyholder lives.

Resident agent *(General Insurance Terms)* — An agent who lives in the same state in which he or she conducts business.

Residual disability *(Health Insurance)* — The portion of a disability that lingers after an insured has returned to work after a total disability. This is usually a partial disability.

Residual income *(Health Insurance)* — A stipulation, usually found in a disability insurance policy, which states that a portion of benefits will be paid to correspond with the insured's partial disability. For example, if the insured now earns 50 percent less due to disability, the residual income benefit would pay half of the total disability benefit.

Residual markets *(General Insurance Terms)* — Markets that fall outside of the usual marketing methods used by an insurer; for example, government run programs.

Resource based relative value scale (RBRVS) *(Health Insurance)* — A scale used by Medicare to determine how doctors will be compensated.

Respite care *(Health Insurance)* — A health insurance benefit wherein the family acting as cargivers to a patient are given a break. The patient is usually moved to a nursing care facility during this time.

Respondent superior *(Legal Terminology)* — A legal doctrine that holds an employer liable for the wrongful acts of an employee.

Restoration of benefits *(Health Insurance)* — A clause that allows an insured's lifetime maximum benefit to be restored gradually after he or she has had a claim paid. This is usually done in small annual increments.

Retainer clause *(Reinsurance)* — A clause that states how much of the insurance the ceding company intends to retain.

Retaliatory law *(Legal Terminology)* — A law stating that insurance agents who live in one state and are applying for a license in another will be given the same treatment as agents who live in that state are given when applying in the state the first agent resides in.

Retention *(Health Insurance/Reinsurance)* — In health insurance, the fraction of the premium amount which goes toward administrative costs. In reinsurance, this term refers to the amount of the insurance kept by the ceding company instead of being re-insured.

Retention of risk *(General Insurance Terms)* — One of the major risk management techniques. This is done by assuming responsibility for the total amount of the risk instead of insuring against it.

Retirement annuity *(Life Insurance)* — A deferred annuity wherein consideration is paid in installments until reaching a pre-selected retirement age.

Retirement income policy *(Life Insurance)* — An endowment in which the benefit is a fraction of the life insurance policy's face amount before the insured reaches retirement age.

Retroactive conversion *(Life Insurance)* — A conversion wherein a term life policy is converted to a cash value form, with the effective date the same as the date the policy was issued, instead of the actual date the conversion was made. In so doing, the cash value policy will be as old as the policy was.

Retroactive date *(Liability Insurance)* — A date that may exist in a claims made policy. If this date does exist, it represents the beginning of coverage. No claims made after this date will be honored.

Retrocession *(Reinsurance)* — A transaction wherein a reinsurer cedes the reinsurance he or she has assumed to another reinsurer.

Retrocessionaire *(Reinsurance)* — The insurer who reinsures a reinsurer.

Retrospective premium *(General Insurance Terms)* — The last premium paid on a retrospective rating plan.

Retrospective rate derivation *(Health Insurance)* — A type of rating system wherein an employer pays a fraction of the employee's cost for health care. The insurer may have to refund some of the money paid, if the costs for health care turn out to be less than the amount the employer has agreed to pay.

Retrospective rating *(General Insurance Terms)* — A type of plan sometimes used when the insured is a large entity. Under this type of plan, the final premium of a policy is not calculated until close to the end of the coverage period. The final premium is calculated, within a certain maximum and minimum, based on the insured's actual loss experience for the period that just passed.

Return commission *(General Insurance Terms)* — A situation that may happen in the case of a policy that pays a commission based on the full yearly premium. If the policy is cancelled before the entire premium is earned, a portion of the commission must be returned.

Return of cash value *(Life Insurance)* — A provision within a life insurance policy stating that should the insured die within a certain named period, the policy will pay the face amount plus the cash value of the policy on the date of the insured's death.

Return of premium *(Health Insurance)* — A clause stating that a benefit equaling the amount paid in all premiums will be paid, minus any amounts paid out in claims, if the claims made in a particular time frame do not exceed a certain percentage of the premiums paid.

R

Return premium *(General Insurance Terms)* — An amount, equal to a fraction of the premium, which is given back to the insured in the case of a cancellation, an adjustment to the rate, or an overpayment of an advance premium.

Revenue *(Health Insurance)* — A term used interchangeably with premium.

Reversionary annuity *(Annuity)* — A contract, called an annuity, which is really more a type of life insurance contract on an insured. This contract only pays annuity benefits if the annuitant is still alive when the insured dies; for example, if one spouse, the annuitant, is alive as of the death of the other spouse, who is the insured.

Revocable beneficiary *(Life Insurance)* — A type of beneficiary that can be changed or revoked.

Revocable trust *(Legal Terminology/Estate)* — A trust that can be revoked by the grantor, who retains control over the trust.

Rider *(General Insurance Terms)* — A document, attached to a policy, that changes the policy's coverage, either by increasing or decresing benefits, or barring some conditions from coverage.

Riot *(Property Insurance)* — An act of violence completed by two or more people. The amount of people necessary to constitute a riot varies according to state law.

Risk *(General Insurance Terms)* — A term used to refer to the person, organization, or thing that is insured. This term can also be used to refer to the outcome of an event, which cannot be predicted, when more than one possible outcome exists.

Risk analysis *(Health Insurance)* — An analysis used to determine the benefits and premiums that will fit a particular group.

Risk and insurance management society (RIMS) *(General Insurance Terms)* — A group that promotes risk management through education, made up of risk managers and insurance buyers. The organization aims to foster better communication between all members of the insurance industry.

Risk appraiser *(Life Insurance)* — The person within the insurer charged with screening new applications. This person is the one to approve or decline the application. He or she may alternately recommend a different policy or premiums to the applicant.

Risk management *(General Insurance Terms)* — A process that involves assessing all possible causes of loss to a company and recommending how to avoid, reduce, or transfer the risk, whether through insurance coverage or through another means.

Risk pool *(General Insurance Terms)* — Also known as a pool. A group of insurers (or reinsurers) who share the premiums and losses of a risk they have written together, according to an agreement that exists between them. A pool often writes large commercial risks.

Risk retention groups *(General Insurance Terms)* — A type of liability insurer owned by the policyholders. The members in this type of organization must be in the same type of business, so that they are exposed to the same type of liability risks. The organization spreads liability equally between the members and offers a different way of financing a liability.

R

Robbery *(Criminal)* — The taking of someone else's property through force or implied threat of force. Robbery is considered a felony crime.

Robbery and safe burglary coverage form *(Criminal)* — A commercial crime coverage that exists in two different forms Form D covers property against robbery or safe burglary. Form D only covers property other than money or securities. The other form, Form Q, covers money and securities against safe burglary or robbery.

Rollover contribution *(Pensions)* — A contribution made up of money taken from a qualified plan. This contribution is then rolled into a second qualified plan. This approach keeps the contribution from being taxed.

Rule against perpetuities *(Legal Terminology/Estate)* — A rule stating that a trust cannot be considered valid unless the beneficiaries get vested in the trust property in the next 21 years.

Runoff *(Reinsurance)* — A clause concerning termination found in a reinsurance contract. The clause states that the reinsurer will be liable for losses sustained under any of the reinsurance policies that are in force, until the policy expires.

R

S

Safe burglary *(Criminal)* — A kind of burglary, wherein property is taken without the owner's consent from a locked safe in an unlawful manner. This is usually substantiated by marks of forced entry left on the safe, or the safe disappearing altogether.

Safe depository coverage *(Criminal)* — Coverage that protects businesses that rent safe deposit boxes to individuals. These forms do not cover financial institutions. There are two forms of coverage for this type of business. Both cover the customers' property while on the premises. One covers the insured for liability costs, while the other covers direct losses.

Safe driver plan *(Vehicle Insurance)* — A plan wherein points are assessed to a driver for each accident he or she is involved in or traffic violations they incur. The amount of points they earn adds a surcharge to the cost of their insurance.

Salary savings insurance *(Life Insurance)* — An insurance policy paid for by payroll deductions, which an employer deducts from the insured employee's paycheck and sends directly to the insurer.

Salvage *(General Insurance Terms)* — Property that an insurer has taken over to minimize losses.

Salvage corps *(Property Insurance)* — A group, created by a property insurance company, charged with limiting property damage due to a fire, whether during or after the fire itself.

Savings bank life insurance *(Life Insurance)* — A type of life insurance only allowed in certain states; for example, Massachusetts. This insurance is sold by a savings bank.

Schedule *(General Insurance Terms/Property Insurance/ Health Insurance)* — A general term used to refer to a listing of the property covered under a particular policy, including the item's description and value. In health insurance, this term refers to a list of medical procedures, whch also states the cost for each procedure. In property insurance, this term refers to a list of the buildings or real estate covered under a certain policy.

Schedule policy *(Property Insurance)* — A policy that lists separately the kinds of property covered, the locations covered, or the different kinds of coverage, along with how much insurance coverage applies to each.

Schedule rating plan *(Vehicle Insurance)* — A plan that permits adding credits or deducting debits from a commercial risk based on certain features.

Scheduled premium variable life insurance *(Life Insurance)* — A type of whole life policy that has a fixed premium amount and a guaranteed minimum face amount.

Seasonal risk *(General Insurance Terms)* — A risk that only exists during a particular time of the year.

Second injury fund *(Workers Compensation)* — A fund established by the state for the purpose of compensating a partially disabled employee who sustains another injury. The fund may pay the entire amount or a portion of the total amount. These funds exist to aid employers who hire handicapped or disabled workers.

Second surgical opinion *(Health Insurance)* — An opinion provided by another surgeon, used to determine whether the course of treatment recommended by a surgeon is valid. This is done to keep the insurer from paying for unnessecary procedures if an alternate course of treatment will have the same end result. A second opionin is required and covered by some health policies before they will cover the cost of a surgery.

Second surplus reinsurance *(Reinsurance)* — Reinsurance that a second reinsurer accepts through a surplus treaty. The amount is equal to the difference between the original reinsurer's retention and the total limit of the first treaty.

Secondary beneficiary *(Life Insurance)* — A person designated to receive the benefits of a policy if the person named as a beneficiary has died before collecting or if some payout remains when the first beneficiary dies.

Secondary care *(Health Insurance)* — Medical care from doctors who do not see a patient at his or her initial visit. Patients usually have to be referred to these providers by a primary care physician.

Secondary coverage *(Health Insurance)* — Coverage for charges that are not covered by a primary policy.

Section 125 plan *(Health Insurance)* — A plan named after the section of the IRS tax code that permits employee contributions the ability to be matched by pre-tax dollars. This is a flexible benefit plan.

Securities *(General Insurance Terms)* — A general term used to refer to the evidence of ownership of a stock or bond. This can equally be evidence of a debt.

Securities Act of 1933 *(General Insurance Terms)* — A law passed in 1933 mandating that a prospectus, a document with detailed information about the company and its finances, must be used in the sale of securities. This act also mandates full and fair disclosure throughout the sale.

Securities deposited with others coverage form *(Criminal)* — A commercial crime form that covers securities deposited with an institution, such as a bank or trust company, or a trusted individual, such as a stockbroker. This form covers loss due to disappearance, destruction, or theft.

Securities Exchange of 1934 *(General Insurance Terms)* — A law passed in 1934 stating that any company or agent who wishes to sell securities must register with the federal government to do so.

Selection *(General Insurance Terms)* — The choice made by an insurer, or an underwriter on behalf of an insurer, of which risks to insure.

Selection of risk *(General Insurance Terms/Reinsurance)* — A general term used to refer to the insurer's selection of which risks to insure. In reinsurance, this term refers to the act of ceding poor risks to a reinsurer and keeping the more desirable risks.

Self administered trustee plan *(Pensions)* — A retirement plan administered by a trustee. In this type of plan, the trustee receives the contributions, invests the money received, collects the profits, and pays benefits to the employees eligible to receive them.

Self funded plan *(Health Insurance/Life Insurance)* — A plan wherein eligible claims are paid by an employer, rather than by an insurer. This is usually only done in the case of an employer whose claim costs remain fairly steady and easy to predict.

Self inflicted injury *(Health Insurance)* — An injury the insured has inflicted upon him or herself.

Self-insurance *(General Insurance Terms)* — An alternative to insurance through an insurer that is generally only available to very large organizations. A self-insured company must make arrangements to meet future risks by setting aside enough money for the anticipated losses and even those that cannot be anticipated.

Self insured retention (SIR) *(General Insurance Terms)* — The fraction of a risk that the insured assumes him or herself. This fraction may be the deductible, it may be the uninsured portion, or it may be self-insured.

Self reinsurance *(Reinsurance)* — An alternative to purchasing reinsurance. This is done by an insurer who creates a fund used to pay for losses beyond normal means.

Separate account *(Pensions/Annuity/Life Insurance)* — A company that holds assets for the participants in a variable contract. This type of company is typically a unit investment trust that has registered with the Seecurities and Exchange Commission.

Service area *(Health Insurance)* — The area a health care plan is allowed to service. This area is set by the state regulatory agencies.

Service benefits *(Health Insurance)* — Benefits provided by a service association. These benefits are issued according to days of coverage, instead of the maximum dollar amount as is done by an insurer.

Service plans *(Health Insurance)* — A type of plan wherein services provided are considered the benefit, instead of a monetary benefit.

Settlement *(General Insurance Terms/Legal Terminology)* — A general term used to refer to a benefit or payment, agreed upon by both parties of a policy. This term can also refer to an agreement settled upon by the parties to a litigation before a verdict can be rendered. This agreement must be mutually agreeable to all parties involved, and may need to be approved by the court.

Settlement options *(Life Insurance)* — Alternatives to a lump sum payment of a policy's payout.

Shock loss *(General Insurance Terms)* — A loss of such significance that the insurer or underwriting company is affected.

Shoppers guide *(Health Insurance/Life Insurance)* — Also called a buyer's guide. A guide to the type of coverage offered, intended to assist the public in deciding on a type of coverage and what policy is best.

Short rate cancellation *(General Insurance Terms)* — A type of cancellation wherein the insured is not refunded in proportion to the amount of coverage days left in the policy's term. The end result of this is the insured paying more for the days of coverage they receive than they would have if they had kept the policy all along.

Short rate premium *(General Insurance Terms)* — The premium associatd with a policy issued for a shorter than usual policy term.

Short term disability income policy *(Health Insurance)* — A policy that provides disability income for a short term period, which is usually defined as less than two years.

Short term disability insurance *(Health Insurance)* — A type of disability policy, issued to either a group or an individual, which typically covers disabilities that last between 13 and 26 weeks.

Short term policy *(General Insurance Terms)* — A policy written for a shorter term than average.

Sickness *(Health Insurance)* — A general term used to refer to physical illness or disease. This term does not include mental illness.

Sickness insurance *(Health Insurance)* — Health insurance form that covers losses caused by illness or disease.

Sidetrack agreement *(Liability Insurance)* — An agreement made between a railroad and a property owner on whose property the railroad has built a sidetrack. This agreement usually states, among other things, that the property owner will not hold the railroad liable for losses caused by accidents.

Simplified employee pension plan *(Pensions)* — Sometimes referred to as a SEP. A type of pension plan in which the employer contributes toward an employee's IRA.

Sine qua non rule *(Liability Insurance)* — A rule that states that a person cannot be held liable for a loss caused by his or her behavior if the loss would have occurred regardless.

Single carrier replacement *(Health Insurance)* — A term used to refer to a single insurance carrier replacing multiple carriers.

Single interest policy *(Property Insurance)* — A policy that only protects the interests of one of the people or entities having an interest in a property.

Single limit *(General Insurance Terms)* — A general term used to refer to coverage expressed as a single amount or single limit.

Single premium funding method *(Pensions)* — A method used to save money to be used toward future benefit payments. Under this method, the money needed to pay out the benefits each year is paid to an insurer or a trust fund on an annual basis.

Single premium policy *(Life Insurance)* — A policy paid through a single premium payment at the beginning of the term, rather than premiums paid over a longer period of time.

Single premium whole life *(Life Insurance)* — A policy that is fully paid through one payment, made at the time of purchase.

Sinkhole collapse *(Property Insurance)* — A peril caused by earth movement that consists of a sudden collapse of land into an empty space under the ground. This peril may be covered by a commercial property form.

Sistership exclusion *(Liability Insurance)* — An exclusion that prevents coverage of products withdrawn from the market.

Skilled nursing care *(Health Insurance)* — Daily care that must be provided by a certified professional. This may include providing medication and treating existing conditions.

Skilled nursing facility (SNF) *(Health Insurance)* — A facility that provides therapy and nursing care to patients covered by Medicare.

Slander *(Legal Terminology)* — A statement that is found to be injurous to the person it was said about.

Sliding scale commission *(Reinsurance)* — Commission paid by a ceding insurer to a reinsurer, which is calculated by a formula. Under this formula, the commission is dependent on the loss ratio.

Slip *(General Insurance Terms)* — A term used within Lloyd's of London for a piece of paper identifying the syndicate who has accepted a risk. This paper is submitted by a broker to the Lloyd's underwriters.

Small group pooling *(Health Insurance)* — A process used for small group businesses, wherein they combine into one pool to receive more accurate rates.

Smoke damage *(Property Insurance)* — Damages caused by the smoke produced by a fire, but not the actual fire.

Social health maintenance organization *(Health Insurance)* — A Health and Human Services funded funded project, which combines adult day care, transcription, and acute and long-term care.

Social insurance *(General Insurance Terms)* — Legally mandated insurance that provides basic economic security for a population. It mostly provides coverage for loss of income due to illness, old age, and unemployment. In the United States, social security can be considered a form of social insurance.

Social security *(General Insurance Terms)* — A general term used to refer to the programs mandated by the Social Security Act of 1935. With the amendments made to the act since then, it is now sometimes called Old Age, Survivors, Disability, and Health Insurance. Through social security, programs that provide assistance to certain segmentds of the public are administrated, such as Public Assistance.

Social security rider *(Health Insurance)* — A rider attached to certain disability income policies that may provide additional benefits, contingent on the amount paid out by Social Security.

Social security tax *(Health Insurance)* — The tax paid by employers and employees that is used to fund social security programs.

Society of insurance research *(General Insurance Terms)* — A group that promotes insurance research and the exchange of ideas between researchers.

Sole proprietorship *(General Insurance Terms)* — A business owned by one person. This person acts as a manager and an employee.

Sole proprietorship insurance *(Health Insurance/Life Insurance)* — Insurance that covers problems specific to sole proprietorships, specifically having to do with the continuity of the business.

Solicitor *(General Insurance Terms)* — A person appointed by an agent to seek out and receive applications for new insureds as a representative of the agent. A solicitor must be licensed but does not hold the power to issue coverage.

Solvency *(General Insurance Terms)* — The ability of an insurer to cover their liabilities and meet the financial requirements of doing insurance business.

Sonic boom *(Property Insurance)* — A potential cause of property damage, caused by an aircraft or other form of air transport traveling faster than the speed of sound, which results in shock waves. Losses due to the effects of a sonic boom are usually covered by homeowners insurance or commercial property insurance.

Special acceptance *(Reinsurance)* — Acceptance of a risk that would not automatically be accepted through a reinsurance contract. This is done through a separate agreement.

Special agent *(General Insurance Terms)* — A general term used for the agent who represents an insurer in a particular territory. In different kinds of insurance, this person may be given a different title; for example, a sales representative. This person is charged with servicing the insurer's agents.

Special auto policy *(Vehicle Insurance)* — A kind of automobile insurance policy that is no longer used. Under this type of policy, bodily injury and property damage have a particular limit of liability, and medical payments have a different limit.

Special building form *(Property Insurance)* — A form once used for commercial buildings, which is now mostly obsolete due to the Building and Personal Property Coverage Form. Under this form, a commercial building was covered against all perils, minus certain exclusions.

Special coverage form *(Property Insurance)* — A classification given to any of the property forms, be they personal or commercial, which covers all risks. These forms offer broad coverage but have many exclusions.

Special multi peril (SMP) *(Liability Insurance)* — A type of policy mostly replaced by modern commercial forms. This policy eliminated the need for several contracts by combining their coverages into one policy. The policy could be changed to meet the needs of each insured, but liability and property coverage was a required part of the package.

Special peril insurance *(Property Insurance)* — Insurance that only covers the items named in the contract.

Special personal property form *(Property Insurance)* — A form mostly replaced by the Building and Personal Property Coverage Form. This form covers the contents of commercial risks against all perils.

Special power of appointment *(Estate)* — Interest in property which has been appointed by a donee.

Specific insurance *(Property Insurance)* — A policy whose coverage is specific to one property. If a property is covered by specific insurance and a blanket policy that covers more than one location, the specific insurance would be the primary insurance.

Specified causes of loss *(Vehicle Insurance)* — A physical damage commercial coverage that is a little narrower than comprehensive coverage. Under this kind of coverage, only specified perils, such as flood, vandalism, or hail are covered. Damage done to a form of conveyance moving the covered vehicle is also covered.

Speculative risk *(General Insurance Terms)* — A type of risk not typically insurable, as it is not possible to predict whether it will succeed or fail.

Spendthrift clause *(Life Insurance)* — A clause that stops a beneficiary's creditors from collecting out of the benefits before the beneficiary recives them. This clause exists to prevent creditors from demanding the insurer pay them the benefit directly.

Split dollar coverage *(General Insurance Terms)* — A general term used to refer to a plan wherein the employer and employee share the costs of the premium. How the premium is divided can vary based on the type of policy.

Split dollar plan *(Life Insurance)* — A life insurance contract purchased jointly by the employer and employee. They share the costs of the premiums and any benefits paid out.

Split life insurance *(Life Insurance)* — Insurance that is partially an installment annuity and partially term insurance. In this type of insurance, the premium amount paid determines the amount of insurance the annuitant can purchase. This is a one-year term policy that can be placed on anyone's life.

Split limit *(General Insurance Terms)* — A general term used to refer to coverage which is divided into separate amounts according to type of loss.

Sponsor plan *(Pensions)* — A term used to refer to an employer that sets up or perpetuates a plan for its employee's benefit. This term can also be used to refer to an employee group that does the same.

Spread loss reinsurance *(Reinsurance)* — A type of excess loss reinsurance. In this type of reinsurance, each year's premium rate is established based on the amount of excess losses the ceding insurance company has sustained during the past years.

Sprinkler leakage insurance *(Property Insurance)* — Insurance that covers water damage due to a leak in the sprinkler system, but not due to the sprinkler being discharged due to a fire.

Sprinkler leakage legal liability insurance *(Property Insurance/Liability Insurance)* — Insurance that protects the insured from being liable in the case of a sprinkler leak that causes damage to those who own property underneath or next door to the leak's location.

Stacking of limits *(Legal Terminology)* — A legal term referring to using the limits of multiple policies to one claim or event. This can be done if more than one policy covers a loss.

Staff model HMO *(Health Insurance)* — A type of HMO wherein all premiums are paid directly to the HMO, which hires physicians. The physicians are then paid a salary and predetermined bonuses.

Standard annuity table *(Pensions)* — A mortality table on which most annuities are based, formally called The 1937 Standard Annuity Table.

Standard class rate *(Health Insurance)* — A rate used to calculate group demographic information. The rate is determined by multiplying a base rate for each participant by a certain factor.

Standard exception *(Workers Compensation)* — An employee or class of employees that are not included the standard classification of a risk. These workers are classed and rated separately.

Standard policy *(General Insurance Terms)* — A general term used to refer to insurance written on a standard risk. This term can also refer to a policy that is standardized to have the same limitations and exceptions, regardless of which insurer issues it.

Standard premium *(Liability Insurance/Workers Compensation)* — A premium amount found by calculating the regular rates on an insured's payroll. This amount is the standard premium, from which a fraction is taken and used as the basic premium.

Standard provisions *(Life Insurance/Health Insurance)* — A term for the provisions mandated by state law that appear in all policies issued in that state. This term can also be used to refer to the provisions the NAIC requires in all group life contracts.

Standard risk *(Life Insurance)* — A risk deemed to be average because it is the same as those on which the rate was based.

State agent *(General Insurance Terms)* — A term, no longer commonly used, for an agent who works exclusively in a particular area made up of one or several states.

State associations of insurance agents *(General Insurance Terms)* — The associations that exist in every state, made up of insurance agents who come together to promote agencies and work on frequently occuring problems.

State death taxes *(Estate)* — A state tax assessed to a beneficiary who receives property from a deceased person.

State fund *(General Insurance Terms)* — A fund established by the state's government to finance a type of legally mandated insurance; for example, workers compensation.

Stated amount *(Property Insurance)* — The amount shown on an insurance policy. It is the amount both parties to the contract have agreed will be paid should a total loss occur.

Statement of policy information *(Life Insurance)* — A document issued each year for each universal life policy. The document details any transactions made over the last year that affected the policy; for example, interest credited and premiums paid.

Statement of values *(Property Insurance)* — A declaration of the value held at each location to be insured under a blanket policy. This is done to determine the amount of the blanket rate to be applied to the policy.

Statewide average weekly wage *(Workers Compensation)* — An average wage calculation, updated regularly, which is used to establish the amount of compensation benefits.

Statute of frauds *(Legal Terminology)* — A statute that mandates certain contracts to be written to be enforced by the law.

Statute of limitation *(Legal Terminology)* — The amount of time a person has to begin legal action.

Statutory *(General Insurance Terms)* — Mandated by law or by a statute.

Statutory accounting principals *(General Insurance Terms)* — Legally mandated principles the insurer must follow when preparing a financial statement to the state insurance department.

Statutory earnings (or losses) *(General Insurance Terms)* — The amount of earnings or losses to an insurer, shown on the NAIC convention blank.

Statutory reserve *(General Insurance Terms)* — A legally required reserve.

Step-rate premium *(Health Insurance/Life Insurance)* — A premium increased at certain predetermined times in the insurance policy. This is usually done in connection with the policy existing for a certain amount of years.

Stock *(Property Insurance)* — Materials that have not yet finished the manufacturing process or merchandise items that are for sale.

Stop loss *(General Insurance Terms)* — A term for a clause that stops the insurer's losses at a particular point.

Stop-loss insurance *(Health Insurance)* — A kind of reinsurance taken by a health plan or an employer plan funded by the employer. The plan covers the plan for losses over a certain amount. This is done on a case by case basis or a total basis over a certain time frame.

Stop loss reinsurance *(Reinsurance)* — Reinsurance under which the ceding insurer is covered for the calendar year. The amount of coverage is determined by the losses incurred by the ceding company in a calendar year.

Storekeeper's burglary and robbery insurance *(Criminal)* — A package coverage policy that covers storekeepers against seven criminal hazards. Separate limits apply to each type of coverage, which must be purchased as a package.

Storekeeper's liability policy *(Liability Insurance)* — A policy that covers property damage liability as well as bodily injury for storekeepers. The policy is issued as a package and only covers claims that arise in the everyday operation of the business.

Straight life policy *(Life Insurance)* — Also called a continuous premium whole life policy. This policy extends the premiums over the duration of the insured's life, up to 100 years.

Strict liability *(Liability Insurance)* — A kind of liability that manufacturers and merchandisers may be exposed to because of defective products they have sold. This liability can apply without regard to responsibility or negligence. To hold the manufacturer or merchandiser liable, the wronged party must prove that the product is defective, which makes it dangerous.

Strike through clause *(Reinsurance)* — A clause that provides a way for losses to be met in the case of a ceding insurer's inability to meet them. This clause holds the reinsurer liable for a share of the losses, which are paid directly to the insured, bypassing the ceding insurer's liquidator.

Sub agents *(General Insurance Terms)* — Agents who do not report to the company directly, instead reporting to other agents.

Sub broker *(Reinsurance)* — An intermediary broker, from whom another broker acquires the reinsurance that needs to be placed.

Subject premium *(Reinsurance)* — The ceding insurer's premium upon which the reinsurance premium is based. This is done by applying the reinsurance factor to the subject premium.

Sublimit *(General Insurance Terms)* — A limit that exists inside another limit.

Submitted business *(General Insurance Terms)* — New business applications turned in to an insurer but not yet accepted or declined.

Subordination *(Surety)* — To give a particular matter less importance than another matter.

Subrogation *(Legal Terminology)* — A legal term referring to the right of someone who has assumed another person's loss to attempt to collect from a third party. This action is not used in life insurance and rarely used in health insurance.

Subrogation clause *(General Insurance Terms)* — A clause that allows the insurer to engage in action against a liable third party to recoup any money for a loss the insurer has already paid. Under this clause, the insurer cannot recoup money from both the insured and a third party.

Subrogation release *(General Insurance Terms)* — A release specifying that the insurer is entitled to the right the insured has to collect from any person or entity deemed responsible for the loss.

Subrogation waiver *(Property Insurance)* — A waiver signed by the insured that relinquishes his or her rights to collect from a third party for a loss. Typically, insurance policies require the insured to preserve subrogation rights. Commercial property insurance policies usually allow a subrogation waiver as long as it is signed before any loss occurs.

Subscriber *(Health Insurance)* — This term can refer to the person who is eligible for enrollment because of his or her job. It can also refer to the person or entity that pays premiums for a policy.

Subscriber contract *(Health Insurance)* — The contract describing the benefits available to each person registered under a health care plan.

Subscription policy *(General Insurance Terms)* — A policy shared by two or more insurers, who each assume a portion of the risk.

Subsidence *(Property Insurance)* — The shifting of the land on which the insured property is located.

Sue and labor clause *(Property Insurance)* — A clause that requires the insured to make all attempts to protect any salvageable property. This clause attempts to make the insured take proper care of the property.

Summary annual report *(Pensions)* — A report that must be sent to each participant of a plan annually.

Summary plan description *(Health Insurance)* — A breakdown of all benefits available under a certain plan.

S

Superbill *(Health Insurance)* — A document that lists every service provided by a certain doctor.

Superintendent of insurance *(General Insurance Terms)* — A title given to the head of an insurance department in some states or provinces. The term "commissioner," which refers to an equivalent position, is used more frequently.

Supplemental contract *(Life Insurance)* — A rider that sets forth the method in which the proceeds of a life insurance policy will be settled.

Supplemental extended reporting period *(Liability Insurance)* — In a claims made liability policy, an option that extends the time in which claims can be made.

Supplemental medical insurance *(Health Insurance)* — A voluntary program that covers physician's costs and outpatient costs, which can be elected as Part B of Medicare.

Supplementary payments *(Liability Insurance)* — A clause found in liability policies under which the insurer will pay certain costs.

Supplemental services *(Health Insurance)* — Extra services that can be added to the basic coverage provided by a health plan.

Surety *(Surety)* — A person or entity who guarantees the performance of another.

Surety bond guarantee program *(Surety)* — A program administered by the Small Business Administration, wherein the SBA backs the surety company should a minority contractor suffer a loss under a contract bond.

Surgical insurance benefits *(Health Insurance)* — Health insurance that covers losses because of surgical expenses.

Surgical schedule *(Health Insurance)* — A schedule listing surgeries and the benefits to be paid for each one.

Surgi-center *(Health Insurance)* — A facility where surgical services are provided on an outpatient basis.

Surplus *(General Insurance Terms)* — The assets of the insurer, minus the insurer's liabilities.

Surplus lines *(General Insurance Terms)* — A risk that cannot be insured by the agents in its jurisdiction.

Surplus reinsurance *(Reinsurance)* — Automatic type of reinsurance in which the ceding company sends the insurer the fraction of each risk that exceeds their retention limit.

Surrender *(Life Insurance)* —The act of giving up a whole life insurance policy. If the insured chooses to do this, the insurer pays them the cash value that has built up.

Survivor *(Annuity)* — The person named as a beneficiary of an annuity contract.

Survivorship benefits *(Life Insurance)* — Funds used to pay annuitants who live longer than is predicted by statistics. These funds are made up of premiums paid by annuitants who died before collecting the amount equal to what they paid in premiums.

Swap maternity *(Health Insurance)* — A provision under which pregnancy is covered to members of a group health plan, but the coverage is terminated at the time the plan is, regardless of whether the pregnancy is still in progress.

Switch maternity *(Health Insurance)* — A provision under which female employees who participate in a group health plan are only covered if their husbands are listed as dependents under the plan.

Syndicate *(General Insurance Terms)* — A group of insurers who insure a high value item or property together. The item receives better coverage through this message.

T Tables *(Pensions)* — Tables used to calculate funding for retirement benefits. Interest, as well as mortality rates, are factored in.

Tabular *(General Insurance Terms)* — A term that refers to anything derived from or having to do with a table. In insurance, a tabular cost is the cost of a claim according to the tables used by the insurer; for example, the mortality table.

Tabular plan *(General Insurance Terms)* — A rating plan that devises a rating formula from various tables.

Target benefit plan *(Pensions)* — A plan that combines a defined benefit plan and a defined contribution plan. Under this plan, the employer must fund a target benefit for the participants.

Target risk *(General Insurance Terms)* — The prospective policyholders, divided by race, age, sex, and other demographics.

Tariff rate *(General Insurance Terms)* — A rate derived from the data in the tariff of rates; for example, schedules and rating tables. This rate is set forth by a rating organization.

Tax basis *(Pensions)* — Money that has not been taxed, most often as part of a qualified plan.

Tax factor *(Liability Insurance)* — A factor added to a premium to cover state taxes.

Tax sheltered annuity *(Life Insurance)* — An annuity wherein the contributions made deduct from the taxable income amount of the employees who participate. The benefits of this annuity are not taxable until they are paid out.

Taxable estate *(Legal Terminology/Estate)* — An amount calculated as the adjusted gross estate minus any marital deduction property and any charitable deductions.

Temporary agent *(General Insurance Terms)* — A person who, without having taken a written exam, is given an agent's license for a temporary period. This period is usually 90 days or less. This type of license is usually issued to a person who is charged with finishing business left incomplete by a deceased or disabled agent, or an agent who has become an active duty member of the military.

Temporary disability benefits *(Health Insurance)* — Benefits mandated by law to be paid to employees who qualify due to a disability not caused by their occupations.

Temporary partial disability *(Health Insurance/Workers Compensation)* — A short term circumstance wherein the person in question is temporarily unable to perform his or her usual duties to the usual extent, but he or she is predicted to recover totally and can work in some capacity until then.

Temporary total disability *(Health Insurance/Workers Compensation)* — A short term circumstance wherein the employee is expected to recover fully from a disability but cannot work while recovering.

Ten day free look *(Health Insurance)* — The right of an insured to fully inspect a health care policy and return it within ten days for a full refund. The policyholder is usually made aware of this right by a notice on the policy's face page.

Ten year funding *(Pensions)* — A kind of funding usually used by older people. The funding mandates that the premiums must be payable for a ten-year period, even though the individual will be allowed to retire within that time frame.

Tenancies for years *(Legal Terminology)* — To have owned a piece of real estate for a particular amount of time.

Tenants in common *(Legal Terminology)* — A type of tenancy shared between two or more people. This occurs when the possession and ownership of a piece of real property is shared among more than two people, each of whom is allowed to sell their share of ownership on the property.

Tenant's policy *(Property Insurance)* — A form of homeowners insurance especially for people who rent.

Term *(General Insurance Terms)* — The length of time for which a policy is valid.

Term insurance *(Life Insurance)* — A kind of life insurance policy that is only valid for a particular period of time. The term length may be measured by years, or can be until the insured reaches a certain age, most often 65 or 70. This type of policy does not accumulate the kind of nonforfeiture value usually associated with a whole life policy.

Term rule *(General Insurance Terms)* — A clause, found within a rating manual, detailing the term during which coverage is valid, and any discounts that apply to policy rates on policies of one year or more.

Terminal funding *(Pensions)* — Retirement funding financed by a sum of money the individual's employer sets aside for them at the time they retire.

Terminally ill *(Health Insurance)* — A status assigned to a person who has been diagnosed with an illness and is expected to die within a certain time frame, usually six months.

Termination *(Life Insurance/General Insurance Terms)* — A general term used to refer to the end of coverage under a certain policy, usually due to the policy's term ending or due to cancellation. In life insurance, this term refers to the end of coverage of a policy due to the insured no longer paying the premiums. In this case the insured would receive a nonforfeiture value, as outlined in the contract.

Tertiary beneficiary *(Life Insurance)* — A person designated as the beneficiary who will receive the proceeds of a policy should both the primary and secondary beneficiaries be deceased at the time the policy pays out.

Testamentary capacity *(Estate)* — The ability of the testator of a will to meet the legally mandated requirements to validate the will.

Testamentary transfer *(Legal Terminology)* — The distribution of the deceased person's estate in the manner specified in his or her will.

Testamentary trust *(Legal Terminology/Estate)* — A trust established in the manner specified in a deceased person's will.

Thaisoi *(Health Insurance/Life Insurance)* — Ancient Greek society that was a precursor to life insurance and health insurance.

Theft *(Criminal)* — A term used to describe all forms of stealing, including robbery and burglary.

Theft, disappearance, and destruction coverage form *(Criminal)* — Commercial crime form that covers the loss of money or securities due to theft, disappearance, or destruction.

Theory of probability *(General Insurance Terms)* — A mathematical theory that serves as the basis for insurance.

Therapeutic alternatives *(Health Insurance)* — Alternatives to certain drugs that have a different chemical makeup, but provide the same result when given to patients.

Therapeutic equivalence *(Health Insurance)* — A term used to describe different drugs that control a medical condition in exactly the same manner as the drugs habitually used to control the condition.

T

Third party administration (TPA) *(Pensions)* — A group charged with accounting and filing reports for qualified plans. This group also acts as the liaison between the employer and the insurer.

Third party administrator (TPA) *(Life Insurance/Heath Insurance)* — An organization that administrates group insurance policies for an employer. This organization works with the employer as well as the insurer to communicate information between the two, as well as processing claims and determining eligibility.

Third party beneficiary *(General Insurance Terms)* — A person who is not expressly named in a contract, but who legally still has rights under that contract.

Third party insurance *(Liability Insurance)* — Another name for liability insurance. It is referred to as third party insurance because it involves the insured, the insurer, and a third party, the person who has been harmed.

Third party payor *(Health Insurance)* — A term used to refer to any company that acts as the payor under coverage provided by a health care plan; for example, Medicare or Blue Cross/Blue Shield.

Three-fourths value clause *(Property Insurance)* — A nearly obsolete clause stating that the insurer will not pay more that three-fourths of the cash value of the insured property.

Threshold level *(Vehicle Insurance)* — Under a no-fault auto insurance policy, the amount at which the insured may bring legal action due to a tort. Often, a no-fault auto insurance policy states that this type of action may only be taken after medical bills exceed a certain amount, or in the case of death or dismemberment.

Thrift plan *(Pensions)* — A retirement plan with an added employee savings feature.

Time element insurance *(Property Insurance)* — Any type of insurance that covers the ongoing expenses created by the damage that stems from an insured loss. The amount of the benefit paid out varies based on the length of time the expenses continue to amass.

Time limit on certain defenses *(Health Insurance)* — A provision that must, by law, be included in all individual health policies. This provision limits the length of time the insurer has to claim that the insured's claim was caused by a pre-existing condition that was not reported at the time.

Time limits *(General Insurance Terms)* — The length of time the insured has to submit a claim and the accompanying documents.

Time of payment of claims provision *(Health Insurance)* — A provision that requires claims be paid immediately, or within a stated number of days.

Title insurance *(General Insurance Terms)* — A kind of insurance that provides coverage to the owner of real property against claims that their ownership of the property is not valid because of mistakes made in the title paperwork.

Tobacco sales warehouses coverage form *(Property Insurance)* — A commercial form that covers operations at tobacco warehouses. The actual tobacco products are only covered during a specific time of the year, and only while inside the warehouse.

Tontine policy *(Life Insurance)* — A policy that was popular after the Civil War, which is now illegal. The policy paid dividends to the policyholders who were still living at the end of a certain period. The money for these dividends came from people who had paid in and were now deceased or who had let their policies lapse.

Tort *(Legal Terminology)* — A civil wrong committed against another, for which legal liability can be assigned. Negligence or acts of omission are considered torts.

Tortfeasor *(Legal Terminology)* — The individual who has perpetrated a tort.

Total disability *(Health Insurance)* — A type of disability that can be defined differently from policy to policy. Generally, this term refers to a disability, caused either by an injury or a medical condition, which stops the insured from working in any capacity.

Total loss *(General Insurance Terms)* — A term used to refer to a claim for a loss equal to the maximum benefit the policy will pay. More often, this term is used to refer to a loss in which the property is completely destroyed, to the point where nothing of value can be salvaged.

Towing costs *(Vehicle Insurance)* — An optional insurance that covers the cost of having a vehicle towed, up to a predetermined limit.

Transacting insurance *(General Insurance Terms)* — A term used to refer to the actual conducting of insurance business, for example, soliciting and negotiating contracts. The definition of this term can vary from state to state, depending on the law in that state.

Transfer of risk *(General Insurance Terms)* — One of the major risk management methods, which is done by reassigning risk to another party. Insurance is a type of risk transfer.

Transit policy *(Property Insurance)* — A type of policy that covers property as it is transported between locations.

Transition program *(Liability Insurance)* — A set of rules within a commercial liability policy. These rules limit adjustments to the maximum and minimum premium amounts due to changes in the rating base.

Transportation insurance *(Property Insurance)* — A policy that covers the insured's property while in transit. All modes of transport required to move the property from one location to the other are covered.

Transportation ticket policy *(Health Insurance)* — A policy that is written in connection with a ticket to travel on a common carrier, covering the insured against accidental death and dismemberment during only that trip.

Traumatic injury *(General Insurance Terms)* — An injury inflicted on the insured's body by an external force.

Travel accident insurance *(Health Insurance)* — A form that covers losses due to an accident that occurs while the insured is traveling.

Treatment facility *(Health Insurance)* — A treatment center that treats patients with substance abuse issues or mental illness.

Treaty reinsurance *(Reinsurance)* — An automatic reinsurance contract that establishes the conditions under which a class of businesses will be reinsured.

Trend factor *(Health Insurance)* — A factor applied to insurance rates to allow for increasing costs; for example, the inflation of doctor's costs.

Trespasser *(Legal Terminology)* — A person who has entered onto another's private property without being given permission to do so.

Triage *(Health Insurance)* — A system, frequently used at medical facilities, wherein people seeking care are ranked according to the severity of their injuries or sicknesses.

Trial work period *(Health Insurance)* — Under social security, a method for injured or disabled workers to reenter the workforce. In a five-year period, a person may work for a total of nine months without losing his or her disability income benefits.

Trip transit insurance *(Property Insurance)* — An insurance policy that covers property in transit during a specific trip, being transported by a certain mode of transport.

Triple option *(Health Insurance)* — An employer plan that offers the employees a choice of different provider types, varying in costs and coverage.

Triple protection *(Life Insurance)* — A kind of policy that comprises whole life and term insurance. Usually, the amount of term insurance is double the amount of whole life coverage.

T

Trucker's coverage form *(Vehicle Insurance)* — A commercial form that provides coverage to truckers who transport goods on behalf of others.

True group insurance *(Health Insurance/Life Insurance)* — A group insurance policy that has been issued with a master contract and actual certificates of insurance, not policy contracts, for each person in the group.

Trust *(Estate)* — An arrangement used in situations where beneficiaries are not yet given control of the property that belongs to them. A trustee manages this property until a predetermined time, where control is relinquished to the beneficiary.

Trust and commission clause *(Property Insurance)* — A clause found in some property insurance policies, which allows an individual to purchase insurance for his or her share of another's property.

Trust fund plans *(Pensions)* — A plan in which a plan trustee receives contributions, and issues retirement benefits to those participating in the plan.

Trustee *(General Insurance Terms)* — The individual who has been placed in charge of the property of another person or people.

Trustees *(Pensions)* — The people who are placed in charge of a retirement plan through a trust agreement made with an employer.

Tuition fees insurance *(Property Insurance)* — A coverage similar to business interruption insurance, specifically for schools.

This coverage protects the school in the case of a loss that closes the school, causing the school to lose out on tuition fees.

Turnover *(Pensions)* — The amount of new employees hired within a certain time frame to replace employees who have quit or been fired.

Twisting *(General Insurance Terms)* — Representing a policy as something that it is not or making comparisons that are not wholly truthful to get the policyholder to alter or switch a current policy.

T

U

Ultimate net loss *(General Insurance Terms)* — The sum that the insurer or its representatives are legally required to pay through legal ruling or settlement. This sum can include medical and investigative costs.

Umpire *(Property Insurance)* — A person used to help a claimant and an insurer agree on an amount of loss for a claim. The claimant and insurer each select an appraiser, and the appraisers choose the umpire. A decision that two of these three agree on is legally binding.

Unallocated benefit *(Health Insurance)* — A benefit that does not have a corresponding schedule of benefits, which repays certain expenses up to a stated limit.

Unallocated claim or loss expense *(General Insurance Terms)* — Expenses incurred by the insurer that cannot legitimately be charged to one specific claim, such as the costs of operating an insurer's office.

Unallocated funds *(Pensions)* — Plan funds that are pooled together to use for the benefit of all the plan's participants.

Underground property damage *(Liability Insurance)* — Damage caused to underground property, such as sewers, caused by mechanical equipment being used to excavate, drill, backfill, grade, or make some other change to the ground around the property.

Underinsurance *(General Insurance Terms)* — A situation wherein the owner of a property or the person suffering a health condition does not have enough insurance to cover the value of the item or the health care costs.

Underinsured motorists coverage *(Vehicle Insurance)* — A type of automobile insurance coverage that pays if the driver is found to be liable cannot pay the full balance he is liable and his automobile insurance policy has paid out as much as it will pay. Under these circumstances, the insurer pays up to a predetermined limit for bodily injury damages.

Underlying *(Reinsurance)* — The total amount of insurance or reinsurance for a particular risk that exists before the next level of insurance or reinsurance comes into place.

Underwriter *(General Insurance Terms)* — A title given to a person trained to assess risks and establish rates and coverage amounts for them. The name is derived from the Lloyd's process wherein each individual who agrees to insure a fraction of the risk writes his or her name under the risk.

U

Underwriter's laboratories *(General Insurance Terms)* — A laboratory environment where items are safety tested.

Underwriting *(General Insurance Terms)* — The act of choosing or denying risks based on their potential insurability to assess them a rate.

Underwriting profit or loss *(General Insurance Terms)* — The amount of profit gained or loss experienced from an insurance policy. This term can also refer to the amount of premiums that exceeds losses and costs.

Unearned premium *(General Insurance Terms)* — The fraction of the premium which has remained unused during the time frame in which the premium was paid.

Unearned premium reserve *(General Insurance Terms)* — The amount of all premiums which have not been earned as of a particular point in time, which is shown on the insurer's balance sheet.

Unearned reinsurance premium *(Reinsurance)* — The fraction of a premium which applies to the part of the policy which has been reinsured.

Unemployment compensation disability insurance *(Health Insurance)* — A type of health insurance that includes coverage for sickness or accidents that do not occur in the workplace. This type of insurance does not cover any injury that would be covered by workers compensation insurance.

Unemployment insurance *(General Insurance Terms)* — An insurance regulated and administered by the government which covers those who have lost their income due to involuntary unemployment. To qualify for coverage under this insurance, a person must work a predetermined length at a qualifying job and earn a minimum amount of compensation.

Unfair claim settlement practices law *(General Insurance Terms)* — A law or multiple laws that exist at the state level to protect the individual in the process of resolving insurance claims.

Unfair trade practices law *(General Insurance Terms)* — A law or multiple laws that exist at the state level, preventing unfair or deceptive practices on the part of the insurance company.

Unfunded plan *(Pensions)* — A term used to refer to any plan that utilizes a pay as you go funding method.

Unfunded supplemental actuarial value *(Pensions)* — The amount by which Supplemental Actuarial Value exceeds Actuarial Asset Value.

Unified tax credit *(Estate)* — A tax credit used to offset certain tax liabilities.

Uniform billing code of 1992 *(Health Insurance)* — A federal code that details the way in which hospital bills must itemize all services provided to each patient.

Uniform forms *(General Insurance Terms)* — A standard form, used widely by many insurers and worded in a certain way. These forms are made and circulated by rating bureaus.

U

Uniform premium *(Health Insurance/Life Insurance)* — A type of rating system used to determine premium amounts. This system does not consider the insured's age, occupation, or gender.

Uniform provisions *(Health Insurance)* — Provisions recommended by the National Association of Insurance Commissioners and mandated by law in almost all areas. These provisions set forth the conditions for individual medical policies, which were developed by the NAIC.

Uniform simultaneous death act *(Life Insurance)* — A law that details how insurers will proceed should their insured and the insured's beneficiary both die in the same accident, in such a manner that it is impossible to determine which one died first. In such a situation, the insured will be presumed to have died first, and the insured's contingent beneficiary will receive any benefits the insured had left to the beneficiary.

Unilateral contract *(General Insurance Terms)* — A contract where only one of the parties makes a promise that is legally enforceable. An insurance contract qualifies as a unilateral contract because the insurer is the only one to make a promise.

Uninsured motorists *(Vehicle Insurance)* — A motorist who possesses no insurance or an inadequate amount of insurance.

Uninsured motorist's coverage *(Vehicle Insurance)* — Coverage found in an automobile insurance policy that covers the insured for damages that cannot be paid by the motorist at fault because they do not have insurance. In such a case, the insurer will pay for

U

the damage done to the insured. This coverage also covers hit and run damage.

Uninsured plan *(Pensions)* — A term used to refer to a plan which is not handled through an insurance product.

Unit investment trust *(Pensions)* — A company investors use to invest in securities. This trust holds assets for the investors but does not do any management duties.

Universal life *(Life Insurance)* — A policy offering flexible premiums. The policyholder selects the amount of premium he or she wishes to pay and the benefits are then purchased in that amount.

Universal mercantile system *(Property Insurance)* — A process largely being replaced by a newly developed system to rate property insurance risks.

Unlevel commission system *(General Insurance Terms)* — A system on which commissions are based. Through this system, the first year commission is a larger fraction of a premium than commissions on renewals.

Unoccupied *(Property Insurance)* — A classification of property, referring to property not occupied by people, but may have furniture inside. This is a different classification than vacant, which means nothing inside the property.

Unpaid premium provision *(Health Insurance)* — A provision that permits unpaid premiums to be taken from claim payments.

Unqualified plan *(Pensions)* — A plan that does not qualify for certain tax advantages set forth within the Code.

Unreported claims *(General Insurance Terms)* — A reserve kept to pay claims that have taken place but have not yet been reported. The amount of this reserve is based on estimates.

Unsatisfied judgment fund *(Vehicle Insurance)* — A fund, mandated by law in certain states, that offers reimbursement to an individual injured in a car accident who cannot collect reimbursement from the responsible party.

Unscheduled premium payments *(Life Insurance)* — Extra payments made to supplement the regular premiums in a universal life policy. These payments can be made at any point in time but must meet a previously set minimum.

Use and occupancy insurance *(Property Insurance)* — An early name for business income insurance. The coverage provided by this type of policy was essentially the same as Business Income Coverage.

Utilization *(Health Insurance)* — The amount of use a health plan gets from a certain group of policyholders.

Utilization and review committee *(Health Insurance)* — A committee that monitors Medicare. The health care professionals that make up this committee observe the medical services and supplies given to Medicare patients.

Utilization management *(Health Insurance)* — A method of assessing the need for certain medical services.

Utilization review *(Health Insurance)* — A process used to control medical costs, wherein the participating employer and the insurance company monitor the quality, need, and suitability of health care services offered by a plan.

Utmost good faith *(General Insurance Terms)* — Legally, the parties to an insurance contract are assumed to have entered the contract in the "utmost good faith," which means they have not misrepresented any facts and intend to abide by the terms of the contract.

V

Vacant *(Property Insurance)* — A building that does not have any contents or inhabitants.

Valuable papers and records coverage *(Property Insurance)* — Coverage that protects the important papers and records belonging to the insured against all risks.

Valuation *(General Insurance Terms)* — A general term used to refer to the approximation of an items value. This is usually done through an appraiser.

Valuation clause *(General Insurance Terms)* — A stipulation listing the value of items. This clause effectively makes the policy a valued policy.

Valuation reserve *(General Insurance Terms)* — A reserve kept in case a liability is found to be valued at more than the estimated value placed on it, or that assets are valued higher than expected.

Value reporting form *(Property Insurance)* — A commercial form used primarily for businesses with a varying amount of value or inventory throughout the year. The business reports its merchandise values at times throughout the year and the insurance is adjusted to correspond to the current value.

Valued *(General Insurance Terms)* — The agreement an insurance company has made to pay a prestated amount should a loss occur.

Valued policy *(Property Insurance)* — A type of policy usually used for high-value items, like antiques or artwork. The policy has a stated amount to be paid should a total loss occur. This is done to prevent the need to determine the actual value of the property lost.

Valued policy law *(Legal Terminology)* — A law stating that an insurer must pay the face value of a policy upon the total loss of a building, regardless of the actual value of the building. The law intends to stop insurers from writing policies in excess of the value of the building so as to collect higher premiums.

Values *(Life Insurance)* — A term used in life insurance for nonforfeiture values.

Vandalism and malicious mischief (VMM) *(Property Insurance)* — A peril that is typically included in homeowners insurance and basic commercial forms. The intentional destruction of or damage to property.

Variable contracts *(Life Insurance/Health Insurance)* — A type of contact that is regulated by both the state and federal governments. These contracts are riskier than the typical contract

V

because they depend on the value of a separate account that serves as the backing for the contract.

Variable life insurance *(Life Insurance)* — A form of life insurance whose face value depends on the value of the products used for equity, such as securities, at the time of payout.

Variable universal life *(Life Insurance)* — A contract offering the features of both a variable life insurance policy and a universal life insurance policy. Premiums and benefit amounts are adjustable, based on the needs of the policyholder.

Vendee *(General Insurance Terms)* — A general term used to refer to the buyer of a property.

Vendor *(General Insurance Terms)* — A general term used to refer to the seller of a property.

Vested commissions *(General Insurance Terms)* — Commissions paid to an agent regardless of whether they still work for the insurer, based on renewal business.

Vested interest *(Legal Terminology/Estate Planning)* — The right a person has to enjoy their personal property, whether now or in the future.

Vested liability *(Pensions)* — The non-forfeitable value of a person's retirement benefits at present.

Vesting *(Life Insurance)* — The right to a benefit, given to a participant because of contributions made by the employer. The participant does not need to still be employed by the employer making the contributions.

Viatical settlement *(Life Insurance)* — A settlement wherein the insurer pays a portion of the death benefits payable under a contract that covers a terminally ill person. In exchange for this early payment, the policyholder gives control and rights to the policy contract to another person. Through this process, the insured is paid a fraction of the policy amount before their death.

Viatical settlement company *(Life Insurance)* — A company aids the insurance company in reaching a viatical settlement with the policyholders of contracts that cover terminally ill people.

Vicarious liability *(Legal Terminology)* — A law that makes a person liable for the acts committed by another person, under certain circumstances.

Vis major *(General Insurance Terms)* — Also known as an Act of God. An accident for which no one person can be blamed.

Vision care coverage *(Health Insurance)* — A type of health insurance plan under which vision care, such as eye examination, and vision aids, such as glasses or contacts, are at least partially covered.

Void *(Legal Terminology)* — A policy no longer enforceable.

Voidable *(General Insurance Terms)* — A policy that can be voided by either of the parties to the contract.

V

Voluntary compensation insurance *(Workers Compensation)* — A type of coverage, similar to workers compensation, which provides benefits in situations where workers compensation may not.

Voluntary employee beneficiary association (VEBA) *(Health Insurance)* — A type of trust used to fund health care ahead of it being needed.

Voluntary reserve *(General Insurance Terms)* — A reserve not legally mandated.

W

Wage indexing *(Estate)* — A cost of living increase available under social security.

Waiting period *(Health Insurance)* — Also known as the elimination period. The time between a disability's inception and the start of benefits from disability insurance.

Waiver *(General Insurance Terms/Legal Terminology)* — An added portion of the contract that waives liability if the injury occurs due to a particular cause or a certain sickness. This term can also refer to a contract stipulation or waiver stating that premium payments are not required if the insured is affected by a disability for a period of time. This term can also refer to the relinquishing of an existing privilege.

Waiver of coinsurance *(Property Insurance)* — Clause that states that the coinsurance requirement will not be considered in effect.

Waiver of premium *(Life Insurance)* — A provision stating that coverage will continue without premiums being paid should the insured become totally disabled.

Waiver of restoration premium *(General Insurance Terms)* — A clause stating that coverage can be restored without a restoration premium being paid.

War clause *(Health Insurance/Life Insurance)* — A stipulation that releases the insurer from liability if the loss occurs as a result of an act of war.

War risk insurance *(General Insurance Terms)* — Insurance that covers damages caused by war.

Warehouse and custom bond *(Surety)* — A bond issued to guarantee the payment of customs fees.

Warehouse to warehouse coverage *(Property Insurance)* — A stipulation, mostly found in marine coverage forms, which extends the policy to provide coverage from the shippers warehouse to the consignee's warehouse.

Warehousemen's legal liability *(Liability Insurance)* — Insurance that covers loss or damage of property stored in a warehouse, in the event of a liability claim.

Warranty *(Legal Terminology)* — A statement made on an insurance application said to be true in every way. If this statement is found to be untrue, the contract can be voided.

Warranty policy *(Property Insurance)* — A policy that provides assurance that a company's warranty policy will remain the same, written by a reputable company.

Warsaw Convention *(General Insurance Terms)* — An agreement between nations establishing limits to the amount of liability a company will be obligated to pay for bodily injury or death stemming from injuries incurred on an international flight.

Watchman warranty clause *(Property Insurance)* — A clause that provides a reduced rate for a burglary or fire insurance policy due to a watchman being on duty.

Watchperson *(Criminal)* — An employee charged with taking care of an insured premises and the property within.

Water damage clause *(Property Insurance)* — A clause that provides for coverage of water damage cause by certain causes.

Water damage legal liability insurance *(Liability Insurance)* — Insurance that covers losses to the property of the insured's neighbors caused by water damage. This kind of coverage usually only applies to the people who live underneath the insured or next door.

Wave damage insurance *(Property Insurance)* — Insurance that covers damage to the insured's property caused by waves or tides.

Wear and tear exclusion *(Property Insurance)* — An exclusion that makes losses due to normal wear and tear ineligible.

Wedding presents floater *(Property Insurance)* — A temporary form that covers wedding presents for a set period of time.

Weekly premium insurance *(Health Insurance/Life Insurance)* — A policy wherein the agent makes a personal visit to the insured's home to collect the premium. These types of policies are usually only for small amounts.

While clauses *(Property Insurance)* — A clause stipulating that coverage will be suspended while certain things are happening at the property.

Whole dollar premium *(General Insurance Terms)* — A premium rounded to the nearest dollar, giving the insured a round number to pay each month.

Whole life insurance *(Life Insurance)* — Life insurance that remains valid throughout the length of a person's life, however long that may be. This type of policy accumulates a nonforfeiture value, which can be paid in different ways, depending on the type of policy.

Widow/Widowers benefit *(Pensions)* — A benefit provided for the surviving spouse of a now deceased worker. This is provided by social security.

Will *(Estate)* — A plan created by an individual to indicate how he or she wants assets disposed at the time of death. This document is enforceable in court.

Windstorm *(Property Insurance)* — A wind of significant force that is able to cause damage to an insured property. Coverage that protects against the effects of a windstorm is usually included in basic property insurance.

Wisconsin life fund *(Life Insurance)* — A state sponsored life insurance plan, which provides coverage to the state's citizens who request it. Wisconsin is the only state to have such a plan.

Work and materials clause *(Property Insurance)* — A clause, usually found within property insurance policies, which circumvents the increased hazard clause sometimes found in a standard fire policy.

Work program *(Reinsurance)* — A clause found within contract bond reinsurance that specifies that the reinsurance is connected to the principal's total amount of work.

Workers compensation *(Workers Compensation)* — Benefits paid to an employee by an employer who is injured, disabled, or killed while working. Under state law, these benefits must be paid by the employer regardless of liability. This term can also be used to refer to insurance taken by an employer who will pay these benefits on the employer's behalf.

Workers compensation catastrophe policy *(Reinsurance)* — A type of excess of loss reinsurance that primary insurers obtain to cover unlimited medical and compensation liability.

Wrap-up *(Liability Insurance)* — A plan that covers all liability risks, which is usually only written for a large amount. For example, a wrap-up policy could be written to cover all of the independent contractors working on a single job.

Write *(General Insurance Terms)* — A term for the act of accepting an application for insurance and insuring the risk.

Written business *(Life Insurance)* — Coverage that has not begun yet, but for which an application has already been made.

Written premiums *(General Insurance Terms)* — The premiums paid on all of the policies an insurer has written during a given time frame.

Wrongful abstraction *(Criminal)* — A kind of insurance that covers robbery and burglary, usually having to do with money and securities.

Wrongful death action *(Legal Terminology)* — A civil lawsuit filed by the survivors of the deceased against an individual or corporation believed to be in some way responsible for that person's death.

X table *(General Insurance Terms)* — A term used to refer to a table in progress that is not yet able to be used in rating.

Y

Yacht insurance *(Property Insurance)* — Insurance that covers pleasure boats against collision, hull damage, and liability indemnity.

Year plan *(Pensions)* — A year during which plan records are kept. This can be a fiscal or calendar year.

Yearly renewable term (YRT) *(Health Insurance/Life Insurance)* — A term life insurance policy that can be renewed yearly without providing proof of insurability, up until a predetermined age. This term can also refer to a type of reinsurance in which the reinsurer only takes on the mortality risk.

York Antwerp rules *(Property Insurance)* — Guidelines for adjusting general losses by a marine carrier.

Z table *(Life Insurance)* — An early mortality table which showed the actual mortality experienced by those insured by major insurers between 1925 and 1934.

APPENDIX

Applying Insurance Knowledge

Jim Warr
iBiz Capital Group
CEO
www.ibizcapitalgroup.com

I believe insurance companies use misleading terminology for the simple purpose to mislead. For example, there is no such thing as cash value; there is only surrender value. Insurance companies like to tell you not to cancel your policy because there is a surrender charge. For example, your cash value is $25,000, but your surrender value is $20,000, so it appears that if you cancel your policy you lose $5,000. Of course, there is no way to get the cash value, so that number is a figment of their imagination. It could have just as easily been a cash value of $1,000,000. This is just another use of deceptive language.

I do not look at insurance through the rose-tinted glasses of a vendor-trained agent. I have studied not only the propaganda from the companies, but I also use a simple financial calculator to verify the truth. I can back up everything I say with math. I have sold life insurance since 1990. My experience/expertise in the insurance field is all self-taught.

If a person would forget about common wisdom and use common sense, buying insurance via the Web would work just fine. Buy as much insurance as you can for as long as you can for the least that you can. SHOP.

M. Bryan Freeman
Habersham Funding, LLC
President & Managing Member
www.HabershamFunding.com

Having been in the insurance business for more than 30 years, it does not seem like learning insurance terminology was difficult, but I am sure it was tougher than I remember. Still, it is my job to understand even the minutiae, and I am passionate about what I do, so it does not seem difficult.

As a consumer, you should be able to just learn the basics and still be well-versed enough to make educated decisions. Every industry has "terms of art" — words that are specific to that industry and which are usually legally defined. You need not learn all of the terms, but you should take care to know and understand the basics. Learn enough to be able to ask informed questions. And look for resources — like this book — that are designed specifically to help guide your learning and purchase process.

Insurance is necessary because you cannot predict the future and some potential occurrences could be financially devastating. Of course, there are also crucial secondary reasons to hold insurance. For instance, in addition to providing for beneficiaries (personal or business) on the death of the insured, life insurance is an investment for the policy owner too.

Deciding whether to buy insurance for a relatively simple and minor item like your cell phone is probably not something about which you need a lot of advice. However, any major financial decision, including decisions about life, health, homeowners and other major forms of insurance, should be approached in a fully informed way. Just as you would confer with an attorney on significant legal issues or with an accountant about weighty tax issues, you should consult a licensed and well-versed insurance or financial professional about insurance.

Timothy Tracy Jr.
InsuringCT and Gerard Tracy Associates
Co-Founder — InsuringCT & Vice President —
Gerard Tracy Associates
www.InsuringCT.com and **www.Tracyassoc.com**

The insurance industry is filled with acronyms, which makes it very hard for people to understand the terminology. Most people do not understand what a PPO, HMO, EPO, STD, LTD, LTC or ADL is, and why would they? It was definitely difficult for me at first, but because we use these acronyms every day, I got used to it pretty quickly. A good agent will be able to break down the acronyms to explain them to you in simple English.

A good independent agent will be able to help guide you through the process and help you make a more informed and educated decision on the appropriate insurance for you, your family, or your business. When asking questions, make sure to ask about what is not covered under you plan. People tend to assume that their plan may cover everything, and that is often not the case. If there is something that you need covered or something you would want covered, make sure you ask your agent if it would be covered. What may work for one person may not work for the other, so just make sure that you are looking at covering your specific needs.

Also, be aware of insurance scams. There are a lot of them out there so it is important to be a smarter consumer and do your homework on an insurance carrier before buying a policy. We all work hard to build our financial foundation, and it is a necessity to make sure the correct insurance programs are in place to protect that foundation against accidents or disasters. Insurance is your safeguard against suffering significant financial hardships due to an unforeseen event that could occur.

AUTHOR BIOGRAPHY

Melissa Samaroo is a freelance writer who lives and works in Florida.